Pitt Cain

Pitt Cain

The Hunt for Revenge

Grant McDowell

This is a work of fiction. Any resemblance to places, events, names, or persons living or dead is entirely coincidental.

Cover design by Holly de Moissac

Copyright © 2017 Grant McDowell

All rights reserved.

ISBN-10:1539989410
ISBN-13:9781539989417

DEDICATION

To Donna, my partner for every trail in life

CHAPTER ONE

Pitt Cain approached the bridge over the river that divided his land from the town of Emerald Lake. He was driving mad, mad at his wife because she no longer wanted to be his wife. Mad because she felt justified in dating her lawyer now that she believed herself free of Pitt. He was angry about the latest bill from the lawyer, resentful toward the people who automatically assumed the doomed marriage was his fault, exhausted by sleepless nights and too much alcohol, desperately afraid of what might happen next.

Pitt aimed more than drove his 1998 4x4 across the bridge, glanced at the roaring river, and imagined slamming into the bridge and over the edge in one grand exit from all the trouble in his life. But by then he was across the bridge, and somehow the fact that he had not drowned himself brought a little comfort, slowed his breathing, and sobered his mind ever so slightly. Pitt threw an empty beer bottle out the side window. He listened as it shattered into a thousand lost shards, a token of his splintered life.

He was driving impaired, but not for the first time and not nearly as drunk as he had driven many other times. Pitt admitted that this time would not be the last, no matter how often he had promised that he was quitting for good. Forget her. He didn't need her. "She's dead weight anyway," he told himself. "And I'll never forgive her."

In fact, he figured she was likely the reason for his problems. What he needed was to get away from this prison of work and fights and bills. Get away from that woman and her rich boyfriend, and maybe even from booze for a while to clear his head. Get to wild country where he always felt more alive. He could see that country in the distance to the north and west: snow-topped, springtime peaks shouldering broad valleys full of wildlife, beauty, bitter memories, and that old bear.

Had someone asked Pitt about his goals in life, he might have looked away at the mountains for a minute, then stated in a matter-of-fact manner, "To kill the old cinnamon bear, and to find that lake." That the one asking the question might know nothing about the bear or which lake Pitt referred to would have meant nothing to him, for those two pursuits consumed him more with each passing season and motivated him more with each birthday, and he was already a weathered cynic at thirty.

No one from Emerald Lake had seen the lake for which their town was named. Many townsfolk questioned the lake's location; most doubted its existence; none had seen it. Mayor Dobbs had suggested the town might change its name. Who cared, Dobbs argued, that an old, forgotten miner had discovered the place? Why hold on to the past, especially one that no one had seen? To continue the story, to preserve a legend, to celebrate yesterday, this was, he said, to waste time, to fail the future, to neglect the next generation!

Yet every spring, the community of three thousand souls celebrated Emerald Daze with a week of downtown sidewalk sales, a beauty queen contest (the winner being determined by how many raffle tickets she sold), a small midway, snowmobile sprints across a grass field—the snow having mostly gone and the green grass being chewed by the powerful machines. The week's crowning event was a country music concert on Saturday night combined with copious amounts of alcohol.

Pitt usually skipped Emerald Daze and went to the mountains. To him they always looked old and permanent, strong and reliable, qualities he liked because he had met few people who had them. Yet the peaks also seemed young and fresh, full of surprises, qualities he feared but that drew him back again and again and again. The mountains always seemed to stare his way, as though looking for him, as though taunting him to come back, as though daring him to venture further up their canyons. He knew that he would soon return. Maybe this time he would find that place his old friend had told him about; maybe this time he would make sense of his life. Yet it was the wildness of that country that held his imagination—held him like a claw that reached right into his troubled nightmares. He felt changed a little when he got out into the country.

What, he wondered as he refocused on the road to town, did life mean anyway, and what did it matter? Lor wouldn't care if he lived or died. He thought she had been mad at him ever since their honeymoon, if he dared call it that. Three nights in a Motel 6 across the border had not been her idea of romance, but what was he supposed to do? Money was scarce; logging had been sparse. Their marriage had gone mostly downhill from that point. Lor had dragged him to a couple of counselors. She even convinced him to talk to his mom's preacher, and he had gone along with it to shut her up, maybe earn a few points from God, if there was a God, and prove he was a good man and not the monster Lor and her rich lawyer boyfriend were painting him to be.

Sure, Pitt reasoned, Pastor Mike was a nice guy. His Sunday talks had usually been interesting, as Pitt recalled, but he was a pastor and surely not able to relate to Pitt's life. Let the preacher take care of the women and kids, Pitt told himself. He would help himself, and eventually Lor would straighten out and see things his way—realistically instead of through pie-in-the-sky stories.

How could he please that woman? She wanted babies, and he couldn't make babies. Secretly, he thought maybe this was a good thing. He wondered if he could love a child like it deserved to be loved. Right now he had no time to think about that. He had to get to the game. So, once over the bridge he skidded his truck around the ninety degree corner, grinned at his skill, and slammed the transmission down a gear. Roaring up the steep road that ran parallel to the river, he began to imagine the game that would start in just under an hour.

Was he ready? He was always ready for the game. Sometimes he thought the game was his life. But sometimes he hated it, or maybe he was just too out of shape. It didn't matter. Not that he thought about life much or contemplated anything more than he must or allowed himself time to figure out the meaning behind his feelings. He just loved the game. At least he loved the opportunities the game brought his way—opportunities to matter.

Although never a great skater or a skilled puck handler, and therefore not a major offensive threat, his role on the team was to get the crowd into the game and intimidate the opposition. Not that he completely lacked skills, but his ability to wind up and fire cannon-like slap shots, though one never knew where they were going, and his habit of collecting a reasonable number of assists, if not goals, were minor compared to his knack for bloodying an opposing player's face with his bare knuckles.

This he accomplished with a certain flair, first nudging the targeted player in front of the net, thus signaling the crowd, if not the prey, whom he would be stalking. Then he'd catch his target off guard with a stick to the back of the leg, or the groin, or if the opposing player's head was down, belt him with a body check that squeezed an "Ooooohhhhh" from the crowd as though the fans had never seen this move before. Finally, he'd rub his glove in the player's face with just enough force to make a weaker opponent careless about his health. Pitt was seldom the first to drop his gloves, for he, the enforcer of the Blue Dogs, the enticer of the hapless, the instigator of the fan club's bloodlust was good at setting a trap, then letting the other man spring it.

He chose his opponent randomly unless the coach assigned one. Usually, however, the team let Pitt play his own game, partly because no one wanted to be on his bad side. His was a game within the game, and he a one-man team within the team. The Blue Dogs had named themselves after a pet owned by their favorite sports commentator, and since they were at best only mildly entertaining to watch, Pitt's bar fighting skills drew a good percentage of their fan base.

Ten minutes after crossing the river, he parked his truck under the tall painted sign that said "Emerald Arena," a title somewhat befitting his gladiatorial engagements in the building. But to locals in this town of three thousand citizens, the arena was known affectionately as "The Rink."

The Rink was over sixty years old. Various attempts, sometimes extensive and expensive, had been made to upgrade the old facility. The place had a smell all its own, an earthy combination of the famous rink-burgers, the last cattle sale, and aging, fading banners hanging from the rafters over the ice surface—banners depicting championship seasons and local heroes both athletic and administrative.

Pitt had come here so often, for so many years, he sometimes joked that his truck could find its way without him. Leaning back against the truck seat, he rolled down his window, lit a cigarette, and sucked in some immediate stress relief. In spite of his addiction to the adoration or fear of the fans in the rink, he had grown increasingly tired of his fame, if he dared think of it that way. His on-ice reputation was all right in the moment while his adrenaline pumped courage through his brain and his right thumped mayhem into the enemy of the day. But as he sat alone, already thinking without thinking about the potential enemy, already anticipating the inevitable fight and the penalty minutes or possible ejection from the game (depending on which referee was running the rules) Pitt felt something like dread, as though he had no choice any more, as though he needed something else.

He fished a couple of pills from his shirt pocket and washed them down with one last gulp of beer.

Then he noticed Lor and what's-his-name, her lawyer. Pitt had called him "Sweetie" ever since he had accidentally intercepted a note Lor had written her attorney. He'd found the note tucked into an unsealed envelope containing a check for legal fees, the note addressing solicitor Arlen Switz as "Sweetie." Pitt still had a key to the house, a fact no one knew, and occasionally he dropped by, maybe to spy on Lor's business or maybe just to pretend he still had a life. He could not be sure which. But seeing Lor and Switz going together to the game—his game—fueled his anger enough to get him to the dressing room. Maybe he could find where they were sitting, hopefully just above the plexi-glass, and maybe he could fire a puck at Switz's head, and maybe he could make it look like an accident.

The banter of the dressing room died down as game time drew near. Players thought about the game and anticipated getting on the ice, hoping to skate out the pre-game jitters. Pitt taped his wrists and smeared Vaseline on his face. If the opposing player managed to get a shot at Pitt's jaw, the lubricant would help the punch glance off. The team hit the ice, greeted by the roar of its fans and the sound of cow bells, which were annoying but effective noise-makers.

Through the first period the teams remained tied at zero, but by midway through the second, the visiting Green Machine was up by three to the Blue Dog's zero. Time to make something happen, and everyone was watching Pitt. He had picked a target—

a tall, lanky player who, though somewhat awkward and unconventional as a skater, consistently set up plays that concluded in goals. Number 76 looked younger than Pitt by a few years, and he was a little taller and a lot thinner than Pitt's barrel-chested, belly-bulging bulk.

"Time's up 76," Pitt said to him on the next shift, anticipating that his opponent would become uneasy. Most players would act as if they had not heard the threat and keep playing with one eye on Pitt, being suddenly more concerned with dental plans than hockey, more aware of body mass than the scoreboard, more pragmatists than pugilists. Unlike them, 76 spun around, faced Pitt, and drove his gloved right fist, still clutching his hockey stick, squarely into Pitt's mouth. And the crowd whooshed out an "Ooooohhhhh."

Pitt's head snapped back, his lips felt hot, his eyes grew wide, and a life-time of repressed memories compressed into a nonsensical collage of pictures and colors that ripped through his brain. The old rage inside let loose. He dropped his gloves. His game was on.

Number 76 was no pilgrim. His long reach landed a rocket-like punch on Pitt's jaw, but the petroleum jelly worked its magic. Still, the other player kept coming. Unlike most hockey brawlers, 76 had some skills, and he had reach. But Pitt's initial surprise had bloomed into full rage. What he lacked in skills, he made up for in power, and he was steadily swinging the power of his right to the man's belly, eliciting a loud grunt from the other man. Soon they were grappling, Pitt landing short, sharp rights to the chin, 76 hammering lefts to the cheekbone. Then gangly 76 got a leg behind Pitt, tripped him, and blasted him with one final left while pulling Pitt's jersey over his head with the other hand, tangling him into a smurf-like bundle and holding him there. And the crowd said nothing.

The silent crowd was loud in his ears as the fans stared in disbelief at their hero while the linesmen untangled him from his opponent—his would-be victim turned conqueror. But Pitt was not finished. In an effort to regain a little dignity, he swung wildly in the direction of 76, or at least where he thought 76 would be, and landed the punch on the jaw of one of the linesmen. The referee ejected him from the game, guaranteeing a review by the league, which would decide if he could continue through the playoff season. Not that it made much difference. The Blue Dogs were down by two games in the semi-finals and losing the third in a best-of-five series. Pitt skated off, ushered by the one still-conscious linesman, and went to the dressing room. Game over. Season finished. Career . . . well, what career? If he couldn't beat a gangly kid, if he couldn't keep the crowd in the game, if he couldn't be part of his team, if he couldn't get his wife back, then who was he anyway?

His rage and jealously turned toward Lor and Switz. She was the reason his life was messed up, and he wanted her to pay, but not as much as he wanted her lawyer to pay. Switz had taken something from Pitt—something more than the ten thousand bucks already down the legal drain. And this, Pitt decided, was going to cost the lawyer.

Pitt shouldered the dressing room door, making it crash against the wall loudly enough that the silent crowd could hear it, as though it were a final buzzer to the season, as though it were one last desperate expression of Pitt's fighting spirit. But he was far from finished fighting. Feelings he could ignore, but fists he understood. A whistle blew; the puck dropped. Play resumed; sticks and skates scraped. The crowd was quiet. Pitt grew angrier with each passing second. He flung his equipment into the bag, skipped a shower, and strode like a man on a mission through the narrow halls of the old arena and out the front door. Ignoring glances from timid fans seated in the heated concession area, Pitt crashed through the main doors, which remarkably held to their hinges, and reached his truck in several determined strides.

He thought momentarily about the carbine behind the seat. "They shoot gophers don't they?" he said out loud. Too messy. He reached under the seat until his hand closed around the twenty-six he had stashed there a week before, tucking it away because he never knew when he might need a few pulls on the bottle. Now . . . time to wait.

CHAPTER TWO

If alcohol could heal his pain, if violence could calm his nerves, if anger could restore his confidence, Pitt would have been the healthiest, sanest, most assertive man alive. The few times he cared to remember being with his father, alcohol was the main feature of the visit. The longer his old man drank, the more he talked, and the pattern was predictable. First he bragged about his toughness, re-telling his favorite fights in detail; then he complained about religion, declaring he was going to get that preacher for leading on Pitt's mother; next he cried, feeling sorry for himself, blaming his every problem on someone else; finally he fell asleep, his head resting on his chin, his hand gradually loosening its grip on his bottle. The drink invariably either spilled on his trousers, leaving an awkward stain in his lap, or fell to the floor, adding to the boozy smell of the run-down, neglected shack of a house. He had moved into the pitiful place when Amy, Pitt's mother, finally divorced him instead of covering for his miserable, abusive, controlling behavior.

Pitt had learned his lessons well, and now he sat in his truck, and he drank, and he waited. Shadows brought an early feel of dusk to the mountain town of Emerald, and off to the northwest the peaks already looked dark, like sentinels guarding their valleys, like giants staring at victims. The more Pitt drank, the more the mountains seemed like omens predicting something was about to change.

He felt the familiar loneliness that grew as the booze melted his boundaries. Then he saw them coming out of the rink—his fans, at least on good nights. He watched, sliding further down behind the steering wheel, seeing the crowd as it trickled into the dim evening, locating trucks and cars or walking to warm homes with what Pitt guessed might be happy families.

Finally he spotted Lor and Switz. He saw her in his mirror as she glanced nervously to her left and right. She and Switz did something between a walk and a canter until they reached the attorney's car, but they did not see Pitt, crouching behind the steering wheel of his truck, still holding a bottle, the alcohol in his blood easily measurable and well beyond the legal limit for someone about to drive. Switz's car turned right on to the street. Pitt started his truck, dropped the transmission into fourth gear by mistake, and immediately stalled. Finding first gear, he followed Lor and Switz at a distance. They drove through downtown, turned left at the only traffic light in town, and climbed the steep street that led to the community's newest housing development. Pitt stayed well back and watched as they parked in front of a house—his house, a fact that slowly but steadily released a growing sense of rage in his intoxicated brain.

To jump out of the truck, to run up to the car, to grab Sweetie by the collar, to drag him from the car, to beat him senseless, to grab Lor and kiss her good-bye one last time, now that would feel mighty good. But to jump and to run on his unsteady legs would make him look out of control, weak, drunk. So he parked a block and a half down the street and waited as Lor and Switz left the car, she glancing quickly up and down the street, he fumbling through his pockets to find something—probably a key.

Pitt waited and gradually became aware that he had no plan, no idea what he was going to do next. He studied the new, black Lexus that Switz had parked in front of the house, compared it with his old truck—four-wheel drive, two shades of green, original paint on the cab, spray-painted color covering the dented box, red tape patching the broken left rear light, and a missing tailgate. His eyes followed the sidewalk from the Lexus to the house, the house he had built, thinking it would make their marriage better.

"I'm building a house," he had announced one day to Lor.

"How can we afford a new house?" she had asked.

"No worries," he'd said. He had worked late on those nights building forms, framing, and finishing. The building had taken eighteen months of hard overtime.

"I never see you anymore," Lor had complained. "Could we talk?"

"Look, I'm busting my rear to get this done for you. Give me a break!" had been his answer.

As he sat in his truck and watched the house, the fierce edge of his rage was beginning to dull while something else, something that was deeper than anger, something always within him grew in intensity. He waited, for though his brain was not clear about what he would do next, his stubborn will forced his body to act. His large bulk poured off the truck seat as he leaned on the open door; his heavy steps scraped the pavement as he aimed for the house now that the couple had gone inside. Pitt was six feet tall, with reddish-brown hair and a thick beard, broad powerful shoulders, and a thick upper body. He was overweight at two-hundred and fifty-five pounds. But he was powerful.

The thought of Lor sleeping with her boyfriend made him feel sick to his stomach. "Why would she take up with him," he muttered to himself. And he wondered what she could see in him. Pitt missed Lor at night, fantasized about her in the daytime, and hated her all the time.

Once at the door of the house, he reached for the door knob. Locked. He knocked sharply on the glass that rattled to his pounding. A light came on. Switz opened the door and quickly stepped outside, closing it behind him. Pitt could see Lor in the shadows inside with something in her hand—a gun?

Though drunk, his memory clearly saw Lor standing in the meadow holding the rifle, a wisp of smoke rising from the end of the barrel. No, he realized, today she was just holding a phone.

Finally, he heard Switz jabbering at him. "Look at me, Cain! What are you doing here?" Pitt turned to look at Switz, who was four inches shorter and a little pudgy with a button nose, a balding scalp, and wide, over-confident eyes.

"I came to visit my wife and my house, you moron."

"You're drunk."

"You're a moron."

"If you leave now, we'll forget you were here. If you don't, we'll call the police," Switz said in the most menacing tone he could muster.

"You do that, moron," Pitt answered. He turned to look through the window again and saw Lor looking back at him, still holding the phone, a mixture of terror and anger on her face.

As if replying to her stare, Pitt drove his fist straight at the shorter man's chin. The blow crushed the cell phone in Switz's hand and landed high, splitting his bottom lip and knocking him, howling and cursing, to the floor of the verandah. The follow-through of the punch combined with Pitt's dizziness catapulted him on to the front porch swing, the swing he had built as a wedding gift for Lor. It was a gift they had seldom sat on, those few times being early in a marriage marred by alcohol and anger—anger sparked by some dark wound, festering with time.

The swing moved from side to side, the door slammed as Switz got inside, the locks snapped into place, and Pitt felt like sleeping right there on the verandah swing. He remembered a few good moments there with Lor as he looked at the lights in the windows across the street. In those houses, he was certain people enjoyed each other's company. But just then one of the screws that anchored the swing's chain to the beam let go, sending his head and upper body crashing to the floor of the verandah while his feet and legs, suspended comically by the still intact end of the swing, thrust upward toward the beams above. He lay still for a moment, and then, thinking he heard sirens, he got up, stumbling toward his truck.

CHAPTER THREE

The next morning he awoke to the smell of something burning, sat up too quickly, and grimaced as the pain shot through his head. Not fully awake, Pitt looked for the source of the odd yet familiar odor, surveying his surroundings, questioning his whereabouts, re-ordering his wits. Like a lens slowly coming into focus, he gradually saw where he was. He saw the back wall of the welding shop, old cars to his left and right, smoke drifting through the open overhead door, and a brilliant flash of light in one dark corner of the shop—a light so bright it made him squint, sending another shot of pain through his brain.

He sat there quietly, trying to let reality settle on him, trying to understand how he came to be in his truck, parked behind a welding shop, but he could not remember how he got there. And that blank spot in his life troubled him. Looking above the open bay door, he saw the big sign, a sign the welder had chosen for several reasons, reasons that brought a smile to the locals whenever they read the words: "Hot Flash Welding."

Pitt remembered then that he had tried to talk to Lor the night before. Rather, he had tried to maim or maybe kill Switz. He was not sure which. He recalled falling head first when the swing broke, and he buried his face in his arms, which were crossed over the steering wheel. His head hurt.

Somebody knocked on his window, and again he sat up too quickly, and once more his headache pounded like a song with no tune, declaring war on his nerves. Gracie was at his window, her eyes betraying deep concern, her mouth smiling, one eyebrow lifting when she saw his blood-shot eyes and bruised face. She opened his door, put a hand on his shoulder, and asked, "What's going on, dear?"

"Nothin' much," he answered, his tone flat and unconvincing.

"Come in for some coffee."

"Thanks, but I've had your coffee," he answered. He managed to smile a little and followed her to the tiny office in the corner of the welding shop where he uneasily accepted a cup of Gracie's coffee.

"Heard sirens last night and wondered if you were all right."

"Thanks," he mumbled.

"You trying to get back with Lor?"

"Not anymore."

"That was some fight last night. You needed your big sister to step in for you," she teased him and laughed softly as she sat across from him, their knees almost touching. He grinned slightly and looked away.

No one in the world could talk to Pitt the way Gracie could and live to tell about it—no one except their mother at least, but she was gone now. Dead after a tough battle with cancer and years of recovering from even rougher times when she had tried to keep the family together and raise a couple of kids, mostly on her own. Gracie, Pitt's only sibling and older sister by five years, bore the marks of hard years too, her face etched with earthy wisdom, her laugh hoarse from cigarettes and smoke from the welding shop, her shoulders stooped forward under the weight of making a living in a male-dominated business, and her eyes, though framed by a cross-stitch of time, gentle, unblinking, soul-searching.

"So, what's on your mind these days?" she asked and looked at him quietly, waiting, knowing the answer, yet guarding his secret.

"What do you think?" he muttered.

Someone hammered steel on an anvil out in the shop while another worker started welding, sending sparks snapping, making light bolt into the tiny office, causing Pitt to shield his eyes and moan. Gracie closed the door.

"Someone I'd like you to meet," she said.

"I'm not in the mood to meet anybody. I'm mad at Lor, and I hate what she's doing, and I hate

Switz, and I've messed up real bad, but I can't get over her. But I still hate her, and I love her. I'm not ready to meet somebody else." Pitt bent over, grabbed his stomach, sloshed coffee on his pants, and let out a sound like a stifled sob. He did not hear the office door open.

"Is this a bad time?" someone asked.

Pitt sat up quickly and pretended to scratch an itch at the corner of his right eye. But the stranger was already looking at him, and Pitt was sure the man had seen through the charade. The stranger was a medium height, dark-haired male with an average build. Pitt knew he was not from around Emerald because he was not white, and non-whites were easily identified in this little town.

And this man's race was hard to place. He did not appear to be from the indigenous peoples, something Pitt would usually recognize, owing to the fact that he himself had some of the blood in his veins, running through the millennia to him from his father's fathers. Pitt gave the man a long look. He did not trust people, he did not generally like strangers, and today he could barely stand being around anybody.

"Pitt, this is Josh. He's a mountain guide and outfitter. Josh, meet my brother."

Gracie made the introduction, and Josh smiled warmly, revealing crooked bottom teeth, and though he was not more than thirty years old, the crow's feet around his eyes betrayed much time spent outdoors in the sun. He extended a hand, and Pitt ignored it, lifting his coffee to his mouth, keeping his eyes locked on Josh. That was his way of being in control. He would shake hands when he wanted to, not when this newcomer thought it was time. Why pretend he wanted to be friends with the stranger? People just made his life difficult. Josh, seeing that Pitt was not about to shake, pulled his hand away and relaxed it by his side. Gracie sighed and stared at Pitt, slightly shaking her head.

Appearing unperturbed but without displaying any sign that he was nonplussed by Pitt's brush-off, the man standing before Pitt smiled at Gracie and handed her an envelope.

"It's all there," he said to Gracie. Then to Pitt, gently, even somberly, he said, "Things will get better."

Josh turned and slipped sideways through the door. Pitt's stare followed, his mind stumbling through foggy theories of who this man could be. Probably another one of his sister's reclamation projects.

Pitt turned to look at her, and she was already glaring at him. "What was that all about?" she said.

"You tell me," he muttered, but he could not maintain eye contact. He never could with her. For all the time he had spent convincing himself he was tough, he never felt stronger than she, and he thought she knew that. "You taking money from strangers now?" he asked, trying to change the subject.

"Rent. You could've shaken hands at least."

"Hmm."

"You don't have to be rude."

"Hmm."

"He's from over the mountain."

To locals, "over the mountain" meant you were an outsider. The term applied equally to people from the next valley and to those from a different continent. In fact, people from far away who spoke different languages or had different-colored skin were more easily accepted than folks from the next valley. The locals liked their Chinese family, their one Arab and one African family. And they loved their hardworking Filipinos.

But people from over the mountain found this mountain town next to impossible to belong to. One family, the Milligans, had come to town when Pitt was making a pretense of being a high school student. They had a son Pitt's age, a son who had noticed Lor's long, black hair and wide blue eyes. But Pitt had noticed the Milligan boy staring at her, and one day in the parking lot he had approached the other kid, pretending to be friendly until he was close enough to break his nose and order him to stay away from her. The kid never saw it coming. Pitt could not remember his name. It didn't matter. The family moved away after their business failed the next year.

Gracie looked away. Then, as if suddenly remembering something she had to do, she stood and asked, "So, what now?"

"I'm leaving town for a while."

"Why? To do what?"

"Sirens. And I got unfinished business." He shifted in his chair, knowing that she understood what he was referring to, feeling self-conscious because she did, convincing himself he was right to leave town.

"You shouldn't go alone."

"Have to. Old Tom said you have to go alone."

"I'll pray for you."

"Don't bother. God hates me." As he said the words, an old anger grew strong, and he could taste its bitterness. "Why would you worship a God who would let people hurt so much?"

"It wasn't him Pitt. He didn't want that . . . ever."

"Then why didn't he stop it?"

"I don't know, but he didn't start it."

He got up, threw his empty coffee cup in the trash, and moved into the doorway. "Thanks for the coffee. It was better than usual," he called back to her as he walked through the open, overhead door, squinting at the bright sunshine, glancing to the northwest. The peaks were still waiting.

"You're welcome. Take a shower!" Gracie left open the door of the little office and went back to work.

CHAPTER FOUR

Amy Cain had been a strong woman to put up with her husband Malen. He would stay home for a few days and nights, then disappear for as many days as he had been home. And Pitt knew his own behavior had not made his mother's life easy. Since the day as a little boy he had seen her bruised face, he had harbored a secret vow to protect her, but he was not always home when his old man got mean, and often he came home from school to find her soft, blue eyes blood-shot from crying or swollen from beating.

She worked part-time at the cafe, taking as many hours as Walt—who was owner, cook, accountant, and janitor—could offer. She took in laundry and ironing and did whatever she could to keep some food in the stomachs of her two growing kids. Eventually Amy had summoned the courage, the desperation, or the survival instincts to take the kids and leave. Malen, Pitt's father, gave her the last bit of resolve she needed. One night he came home drunk, and he brought another man with him. The man leered at Amy, licked his lips, and told her Malen owed him money but that he had settled the debt in exchange for a night with Amy. Malen, for his part, was sitting stupefied at the kitchen table, his eyes glazed, unable to look at Amy, whose expression changed from astonishment to fear and then to defiance as the other man moved closer and put a hand on her waist in an attempt to pull her close. She screamed.

Pitt could remember every detail of what happened that night. His mother's frightened, angry scream dragged him, still half asleep, from his bedroom and down the stairs to the kitchen where a man was tearing his mother's shirt. At fourteen, Pitt was big for his age with heavy forearms and thickening shoulders. His feet barely touched the kitchen floor as he jumped from the bottom stair, hitting the man squarely in the jaw, jarring loose his grip on Amy. But whoever he was, the man had been punched before, and after staggering for an instant, he drove Pitt halfway across the room and to the floor with a blow to the chin.

"Control your kid," Pitt heard the man yell at Malen. Shaken, Pitt tried to drive back at the other man, but a kick to the stomach knocked him back to the floor. The old man had stepped in, and had he not been so wasted, his boot could have broken some of Pitt's ribs. Instead, his intervention broke open an anger that simmered near but never above the surface of his son's consciousness . . . until that moment.

Pitt's body became an automaton of fury. Oblivious to danger, impervious to pain, he sprang from the floor, driving a fist into his old man's crotch. The old man howled while the young son smashed that same fist repeatedly into his father's face until its lips and teeth were a mass of jellied chunks. His mother's attacker had turned his anger on her and was slapping her face and chest. A blow from Pitt's knuckles stopped him and dropped him to the floor, but not before Pitt crushed his nose with a sharp elbow. Amy prevented him from—albeit barefoot—stomping the man's head into the linoleum, and then she held him and began to sob. Not for the first time, the neighbors had called the police when the screaming began in the Cain house.

"What happened, Mrs. Cain?" It was Constable Molloy.

Amy looked at Malen, and the fear in her eyes turned to calm. "This man came home with my husband, and he tried . . . he tried to hurt me."

"What did he do to you?"

"He tore her shirt. He tried to kiss her. His hands were on her," Pitt blurted out, his words angry and defensive. The other officer moved toward him, but Molloy, older and wiser, stepped in his way.

He said quietly, "Look, son, I think you did what you had to do, and we'll take it from here. Are you all right? You took a rough cut to that eye."

"I'm fine," Pitt answered.

"All right." Molloy turned to his partner. "I think we've got what we need."

The officers left with the two battered men, hands cuffed behind their backs. Amy began packing that night. But leaving home in a town as small as Emerald Lake meant seeing the same people one saw before moving from the family home to an apartment, keeping the same job, serving lunch to the same gossip groups that met daily at the Mountain View Cafe.

Gracie had left home a couple of years before, as soon as she could sustain herself from what she earned welding and waiting tables. Still, the move for Amy was a new beginning, and some people at the Gospel Hall—the little storefront church on Main—were especially kind to Amy and her kids. They offered clothing, groceries, and even a little cash when money was gone and rent was due.

Amy was baptized and became a member of the little group that met in the downtown church. She had peace that Pitt had not seen in her before—peace he could only dream about—and it was peace he could not or would not believe possible for himself. Both he and Gracie struggled to fit in with Amy's new routines.

He might have been interested in participating, as much as he hated to admit so now. Pastor Mike's talks were interesting, and the pie served after the services was worth waiting for. But his old man, never one to miss an opportunity to harass his mother, would park in front of the little church on Sunday. Since he could no longer legally come near Amy's apartment due to a restraining order, a boundary he breached at least weekly and more often after pay days when he could afford more booze, he had become even less inhibited and threatened ever more destruction.

There he sat on Sundays, dark glasses hiding his bloodshot eyes. His dark eyes watched Amy. His dark mood intimidated Pitt, who often veered away from Amy out of either fear of the old man or longing to know him—he was not sure which—and climbed into the passenger seat of Malen's truck. Pitt remembered the old man smiling at him, offering to take him to the mountains to go fishing, ignoring Amy as she stood in the doorway of the church.

"Thought I'd save you from the hand-wavin' pew-jumpers," the old man would say. Pitt would try to laugh. He remembered well those Sunday mornings with the old man. But the memory was all that existed because the so-called fishing trips always ended before they began with a stop at the hotel to pick up some booze, then a drive to the small park on the edge of town.

"This oughta be a good spot," Malen would say, pointing to the little stream that ran through the park, and Pitt would play along. He'd take his old man's gear and fish the stream, catch nothing, and walk home in the evening. Malen would have fallen asleep behind the wheel of his truck but not before he had told Pitt stories his father had told him, stories of the abusive priest in the residential schools from long ago and of hypocrites who told you one thing and did another. Pitt knew some of the stories were true. Eventually he gave up pretending to fish in the little stream and stayed in the truck to drink with the old man.

As Pitt grew older, he hated himself for anything that reminded him of his father. But he would stay out late and come home drunk. His mother had long ago stopped locking the front door. When she and Malen had shared the house, the old man had simply broken the door whenever he lost his key.

When Pitt had met Lor, he thought he could change. He even tried to change for a while, but eventually he gave up, believing he could not, feeling he could never do enough to make her happy anyway.

Relationships had proven complicated, and he did not understand why. "Maybe I'm just not a marriage kind of guy," he sometimes told himself. Maybe, he thought, I'm too much a man's man to be tied to a woman. That, he reasoned, was likely the problem. His broken marriage was not his fault. He was just too much man, and Switz was . . . well he was probably someone Lor could control. "All the best, little man," Pitt chuckled to himself, as he sat in his truck behind the same hotel the old man had frequented.

CHAPTER FIVE

By early-afternoon, Pitt was packed and driving to the mountains, leaving behind his unsolved problems, something he learned from example and a habit that, though he was not proud of it, seldom prevented him from making more mistakes. Well, he had the old man to thank for that, and he had Lor to blame for ruining his life. At least he told himself so.

As he drove to the crest of a hill he caught a glimpse in his mirror of the town of Emerald Lake, a place he had called home but never felt at home in, a community that both praised him and punished him for his transgressions.

"Good riddance for now," he sighed. He drove across the bridge, then turned northwest along the river. The town remained in his mirror for a while, a town that survived on a sputtering logging industry, a little mining, minor deposits of oil and gas, and some tourism for those who wanted a remote place. It was a town of veterans, recluses, runaways, and rig workers, a place fueled by gallons of beer and not a little whiskey. But it was home.

He stopped at his cabin, set back from the river and up a low rise in the tall lodgepole pines. After unlocking a heavy padlock on the door of the only real building on the place, he went inside and retrieved a rifle. This was his favorite, an old 44. The old gun kicked like a mule, roared like thunder, and carried a slug heavy enough to tear up a bear's guts. Pitt slung the rifle over his shoulder, grabbed a box of ammunition, and looked around the little two-room house. Pitt knew that anyone else would call the building a shack. To him, however, the place felt like home, at least more like home than the house he had built in Emerald for Lor, more like home than the empty, cramped hotel room where he had exiled himself.

He thought about coming back here after his trip, moving into the old house, maybe fixing it up a bit, something he had meant to do for years. He shifted his weight, and the floor creaked, the sound reminding him of the old man named Tom he had often visited here, the man who had let him stay, the man who had been more like a father than his own father.

The night that the police hauled away Malen after Pitt had bloodied his face, Pitt had tried in vain to sleep, tried to forget that his father had kicked him in the gut, tried to think of how to avenge his mother. After a couple of hours imagining revenge, listening to the old clock tick loudly in the silent night, and wishing he could be anywhere but where he was, he found himself walking out of town. He was headed nowhere but somewhere, looking for no one but someone, hoping for nothing but anything. He had no idea what time he came across the little house, but the moon was bright that night, and he followed his steps across the bridge, along the river, and up the lane that led to this place.

"Who's there?" he had heard a soft, older voice say. He had not seen the speaker, but the voice was calm and steady.

"Ah, I . . . I'm Pitt Cain," he had stammered, trying to see who was in the doorway of the little house. And as he squinted and focused he saw moonlight reflect on metal, and that was the first time he had seen the old 44, the gun's butt near the man's right shoulder, the barrel pointed near Pitt's feet. The man behind the gun was not very tall, maybe five foot eight, and as Pitt's eyes adjusted to the dim light coming from somewhere inside the little house, he saw that the man had shoulder-length silver and black hair.

"You lost, Mr. Cain?"
"No. No . . . I'm, ah, just out for a walk."
"At 2:30 in the morning?"
"Yeah."
"You hungry Cain?"
"Not really."

"How about some coffee? Looks like your face didn't do so good on your walk."

For the first time, Pitt became aware of his swollen left eye, and his puffy lips. Involuntarily, he felt the left side of his face. During the fight he had not felt any pain, but now his face was throbbing, his gut was aching, and suddenly the warm glow inside the little house and even the man holding the gun seemed like the best things he had seen in a while. He stepped forward. The old man moved out of the doorway to let him in, still casually holding his rifle, his unreadable expression tracking every movement of his young guest.

"Have a seat." He pointed with his left hand to a wooden chair at a small square, hand-made table, and Pitt eased slowly into place.

The next morning, Pitt had awakened to the aroma of still more coffee and bacon. He felt his face, tried to remember how he came to be lying on a narrow bed in a cabin that smelled like old leather, cedar, coffee, and bacon all at once—aromas that smelled like home but a home he had not known. He remembered eating bread and honey the night before between gulps of hot coffee until his stomach filled up and his eyelids grew heavy and his old host said, while pointing to the bed, that he should get some sleep.

The man had identified himself as Tom but had said little more. His small home was furnished with slightly more detail than he had revealed about himself. As Pitt took in his surroundings that morning, he saw a small corner closet covered with a curtain, the table and two chairs, a counter with a sink and a pump beside it, an ice chest, a wood stove, the bed he was laying on, and a two-foot-high cross hanging on the wall above the counter. He saw no sign of where the old man had slept.

"Help yourself," was written in remarkably neat, clear script on a note on the table, and Pitt assumed this referred to the bacon and pancakes still warm on the wood stove. When he had finished his breakfast, he had gone outside, seen nothing of his host, and decided to walk home. And an hour later, when he reached the house, his mother met him at the door, telling him an old man named Tom had dropped by to say Pitt was all right. And he had left a package of deer meat.

"You scared me," she had said to Pitt. "I didn't know where you went." He remembered how she looked—exhausted with dark circles under her eyes, her clothing uncharacteristically unkempt. Boxes were stacked on and around the kitchen table, and most of the cupboard doors were open.

"Sorry," he had said quietly. He gave her a tender hug, but abruptly stopped when she winced in pain, her body still hurting from the stranger's careless, selfish advances.

"Sorry," Pitt said again.

"It's all right," she said quietly. "I'm proud of you."

The deer meat was the first of many small gifts old Tom would drop off. And when he died several years later, having no heirs and no family, he had left his property to young Pitt.

Pitt had always thought that someday he would live on this land, starting out in the little cabin, eventually building a house where he and Lor could raise a family, but he had never forgiven himself for Tom's death, and he was not ready to live in the old house. And today, living on this land seemed like a distant dream, a jaded joke.

He laughed at the idea, the kind of laugh that is part shame, part disgust, part cynicism. Stepping outside, he smelled the same pungent pine he had smelled sixteen years before on the night he met old Tom and his gun. The early-morning air was full of springtime, and he cradled the 44 in his left arm and lifted a flask with his right to his lips.

CHAPTER SIX

Pitt parked his truck at the trailhead. The two hour drive across logging roads, some so long out of use that they were barely navigable, had left his flask almost dry, and he drained it with a quick motion, licking his lips, as though missing one drop would be a grievous loss. Pitt Cain could hold his liquor.

He looked at the sky. Only when old Tom had referred to the sky, or only when it threatened a storm, had he been aware of it, but today Pitt let his eyes roam around the heavens. An "expanse" he had heard the preacher call it one Sunday long ago. To someone else, to someone who took the time to listen to his surroundings, to someone not running from wife, lawyer, and lovers, the wisps of dark cloud might look like frail strands of an old man's hair, badly combed and sparsely spread, swept out from a thunderhead. Shafts of sunshine pierced the high cloud ceiling, forming a bright veil that descended gracefully to the ground, and patches of blue promised the breakup of the coalition of storms and wind that fulminated in the distance. But Pitt just saw bad weather.

He was getting away from it all but felt it all with him, as though a stiff breeze kept pushing him back, like dead weight riding his pack. He needed to get away from work, which had been easy, since his skills as a dozer operator were not required anywhere at the moment. He needed to leave behind the fights and bills, especially the unpaid variety left piling up in the old hotel room that smelled like stale beer. He needed to pull away from Lor and forget what might have been yet could never be. He wondered now, if he had not been drunk when he proposed, could he ever have summoned the guts to ask her to join him in a futureless life? He needed to get away from her and her rodent-like boyfriend who was sure to try to sue him for all he could get. He needed to get away from booze, but not just yet. Like a man carrying insurance, he had brought along a supply of alcohol that was already beginning to feel too small to nurse his backcountry loneliness.

Pitt stepped out of his truck, hoisted his backpack, and slid the 44 into the special boot he had mounted on the side of the pack. Out here he had no worries about meeting wildlife officers who would resent the presence of his gun. In this part of the country, a man was pretty much on his own with the exception of a few other men he might meet along the trail. When he met someone, he felt uneasy camaraderie, uncertainty as to why the other man was here, yet some comfort in the company of a fellow traveler. He had seen a woman out here only once.

He glanced one more time at the sky, then started up the trail. The rain began. Big splattering, orphaned drops alternated with a misty mask of moisture, then humid bands of sunshine, as he trudged forward and upward. The early part of the trail was steep, and as a result of the rain it became slippery. After slogging up and sliding down the undulating land for half an hour, his knees caked with mud and pine needles, his shirt sweat-stained and stuck to his skin, he fell again, hard this time, absorbing some of the impact with his left shoulder and his skull. He pulled on his flask, but it was empty. Just for a moment he thought about digging through the heavy pack for more alcohol, but he was exhausted. He realized that he had not eaten anything that morning, having consumed only the liquor he had carried in the truck. He reached back, felt a side pocket, and dug out a candy bar from the big pack. "Breakfast of champions," he muttered.

After another thirty minutes, a few more stumbles, and a growing, thumping headache, Pitt rounded a corner where the left side of the trail was walled by young, light green, velvety tamaracks. Yet what caught his attention and made him look again was not a tree but a hairy, young grizzly. He had seen the sign—the clawed, bare trunk of a tree seven feet above ground, as if something wanted others to know this trail was private. But nothing ever prepared Pitt for meeting a bear on the trail, and this young one looked directly at the hiker, as though puzzled by and intrigued with the stranger's appearance. The bear's coat was not yet sleek; long, wispy, brown hair framed its face, like that of a boy trying too soon to grow a beard. He had the look of a party-goer who had overslept and arrived late for work, not aware that his mullet was unkempt and comical. The hairy creature might have been funny had it been alone.

"Where's your momma, little man?" he asked softly. He worried about the mother who would see him as a threat to her cub. Pitt reached for the 44 and unsheathed it, and he swore softly at himself when he saw that mud from his fall had plugged the barrel. The old gun felt more like a friend than a firearm to Pitt. It was part of his memory of Tom. Tom would know what to do right now, and he would never have let his gun get clogged with mud, yet Pitt also knew that Tom would have understood how it happened.

Tom had been more a father to Pitt than his old man ever had been. Pitt seldom thought of his father by name and rarely thought of him as his dad. He tried not to think of him at all, usually considering him an embarrassing nuisance, a leaking vault of bad dreams, a memory to flush away with alcohol.

By contrast, old Tom had been the man in Pitt's life. Malen had run from a teenage son; Tom had come alongside. His old man drowned conversation with whiskey; Tom dove into confusion with questions. Malen kicked his son in the guts; Tom had the guts to stand by Pitt's side. He'd done so when the creep who assaulted his mother found Tom's cabin and demanded that "the kid," as he'd called Pitt, come out to face him. Tom looked at Pitt that evening, smiled, and calmly opened the door. He stared at the man, who tried to look past him into the little house but stepped back when he saw the penetrating eyes of the older man and the cool, steel barrel of the 44. He fumed and vented and cursed, but Tom never blinked. After a few moments, Tom held up his left hand and said, "Quiet. I know who you are, Jonas Mulaire. I know you are a snake of a man. I know what you do to women, and if you come here again or harm this boy, I don't mind much where I spend the rest of my days, but that will be your last." And that was the last Pitt saw of Mulaire for a long time.

But his memories of Tom's courage, flashing through his mind in an instant, did not solve the problem of the bear cub. Pitt decided to back slowly down the trail and maybe set up camp in a small clearing he had passed, or find a game trail that might take him around the bear. To spook the cub might draw the wrath of the mother bear, and to surprise her could do the same. Just as he stepped back, still watching the bear as it stared back at him, he saw the sow, not ten feet past the cub, grazing on some huckleberries. Maybe she was one of the old sows that was going deaf. Rangers warned hikers going to the back country to make noise on the trail because a surprised bear is a problem no one wanted to face. But a deaf bear was a different problem, and this one seemed oblivious to Pitt's presence. Not for long.

As he turned to retrace his steps, his toe caught a root on the edge of the trail, sending him down on his side, fetching a loud grunt and an involuntary scream of pain as his ribs, still sore from crashing with the deck swing, absorbed his fall. Luckily, the old bear, startled by the sudden loud sound, bolted away, and her cub followed, both bears pausing to look back before slipping deeper into the tamaracks and away from the trail. Pitt struggled to his feet, spewing angry expletives at his clumsiness but relieved to be alone again. He took time to clear the gun barrel before plodding on up the trail, his gun in hand instead of sheathed. "You never can tell with grizzlies," Tom had told him.

By the time he reached the clearing where he had camped several times before, the late-arriving sun was hiding behind the western peaks, and the cooling air prompted Pitt to start a fire. The picas and squirrels, when they were not trying to raid his pack, were scolding him for disturbing their district. He tossed a stone at the one whose head had disappeared inside the pack, and it clucked its disgust at him as it retreated down a hole at the base of a tree. With a gun or a stone or a fist he could hit most anything he aimed to hit, but when he aimed for relationships he missed, whether with words, or gestures, or anything that required the subtle nuance another person might need.

He laughed at his tent. "Two-man tent!" he chuckled with some degree of contempt, the tent being made somewhere far away by someone half his size. As he surveyed his crude campsite, he felt hungry and pulled a steak from his pack, a tradition he learned from Tom who had always brought a heavy meal for the first supper. "A treat for the trail," he had called it.

Soon Pitt had a fire going, big enough to warm his body but not so big that it charred good beef. It was at that moment, when the steak was hanging on a make-shift spit over the fire, beginning to smell good and increase his hunger pangs that he saw something move down the trail.

"Momma bear, you cannot have my steak," he said aloud, and he grabbed up his rifle and stared through the bush that squeezed the sides of the slim path. He loved these mountains, but the thought of a grizzly coming through his camp still made the hair stand up on the back of his neck. Every time he headed deep into the mountains he felt this way, but every time he planned a trip he forgot about his fear until he was here. The farther he traveled from the people he could not stand, the more fearful he felt of the mountains he loved.

But it was not a bear that came around the corner and into view. Two men stepped into the small clearing. One he knew from Gracie's shop. Josh smiled and nodded at Pitt, his teeth blaring white against the copper-like color of his skin. The other man was much taller, angular, more reserved, and he stared across the fire at Pitt, who gripped his rifle more tightly and merely nodded. The tall man seemed familiar, but Pitt could not say why.

Finally Josh broke the awkward silence, "Mind if we share your site?"

"I'm surprised to see you here," Pitt said. "Gracie send you to babysit?"

Josh laughed, which irritated Pitt, for he hated the feeling that someone was making fun of him, even though Josh offered no sarcastic retort.

"No friend. I'm a guide, and this is Kelly Ludrow. He's a photographer looking for bear."

"Mostly, I photograph them in their natural habitat," Ludrow added in a deadpan tone.

"You alone?" Josh asked. "We saw two trucks parked at the trailhead."

"Just me here. Mine was the only truck when I pulled in."

"Well, somebody else must be around."

"Mm-hmm," was all Pitt had to say. Finished with conversation and not pleased with his company or the idea of a photographer snooping around his mountains, he turned to his steak, lifted it with the makeshift spit and began biting off the rare edges, ignoring the work of the other men as they hurried to set up camp before the next cloudburst.

CHAPTER SEVEN

Back down the trail, another man camped out of sight in a small opening in the trees, and he carried two things that were deadly in the hands of the wrong person: a heavy rifle and an even heavier grudge. He had gone by other names in other places, but he was content, at this point, to use his own name; he had gone by his real name so seldom that not many knew what it was.

A cunning and malicious man, he had a well-defined goal wherever he went—cause instability and then move on. He had been a crook since his youth, and he had come to believe that society owed him a living, that individuals and communities ought to give him his share. At first he had worked at various odd jobs while supplementing his income with petty theft, pawning stolen items, or stealing cash when he could. Then he graduated to more complex plots. Finally, he had joined the gang, or the brotherhood, as they liked to think of themselves.

But he was now into his forties, and he had developed more refined tastes, preferring roles that gave him access to a credible lifestyle and that covered his mean streak. He was a mechanic by trade, but he did not like getting dirty. One of his clients had discovered that he had charged for work he did not do and parts he did not install. The client became his first murder victim, carefully disposed of in an abandoned well before he could talk about the mechanic that cheated him.

He was pleased at how easily the killing had gone, how quietly and efficiently. That was the first of seven, each one carried out with meticulous care. Although he was a killer, he was also a perfectionist, taking time to plan a killing, moving to another part of the country, and then returning quietly in disguise to do the job. His victims were people who obstructed his plans. He had killed a local politician, a nosy lawyer, a troublesome school board chair, a preacher—a death that had bothered him for nearly a week—and others. But this time he had come back to Emerald to settle an old score that was more personal. He was sure of himself. He felt somewhat invincible; he had never botched a job.

Anyway, the community would be happy when it was done, because everyone he listened to seemed fed up with Pitt Cain. Well, everyone except Pitt's sister, and the killer was not sure about this character that called himself Josh. This was one man he could not see through. As for the tall, lanky fellow on the trip, he might end up as collateral damage.

This time he might just stick around and listen to the scuttlebutt going around about how Pitt finally bought it. It could be fun. To stay in the mountain town, to have a permanent address, to play the part of the righteous might be a good idea. He would ease out of attending the little church, and he could stay away from Gracie. To use religion as a cover was one thing; to weekly face so many sincere folks would be another.

Yes, if this job went right, if he could eliminate the only man who might reveal his past, if he could clean up this one detail, he would settle down in Emerald. He would stay close to the land he knew. He would live simply but well on the generous trust of suckers he had tricked and whose money he had taken. He would keep his real name, which not even his gang-member brothers knew.

Besides Pitt, only one other man knew of his history. Only one knew how efficient and deadly he could be, how well his manners concealed his malevolence, how quickly his smooth talk deceived the forgiving. But because that man feared him—not only for what he might do but also for what this killer knew of him—he would keep quiet, or his own past would be exposed, and he would certainly die.

That man was Arlen Switz. He had been the murderer's lawyer, helping crimes look legal for a decade. Besides paying his lawyer well, the murderer would refer potential clients to Switz—clients who were unhappy with husbands or hurting from abuse. Ever the compassionate advocate, their new attorney would listen, humbly receive a retainer, and pursue with passion those he found attractive. The man now hidden down the trail from Pitt had told Switz, having heard the coffee-shop news, that the gorgeous Lorelai Cain was unhappy and angry. And he had hinted that Emerald might be a good little place to live for reasons of business and privacy.

Yet someone, or rather something else, was also paying attention to the travels of Pitt Cain. Her aging eyes less useful now, her hair more shaggy, her bulk more imposing, she sensed more than saw the coming storm. And was there something else in the breeze that whistled a shrill song in the tall trees around her, something old, familiar, even dangerous? To the old bear, life was simple—eat, survive, protect your territory, and occasionally kill. She remembered this scent, and it made her wary.

CHAPTER EIGHT

The tall man at the fire with Josh had looked familiar, but Pitt could not figure out why. Cocooned in his sleeping bag, he puzzled over the lanky character until he fell asleep. He lay dreaming of the last hockey game, feeling suffocated by his own hockey jersey, and then awakening with a groan that in his dream was a loud roar. He took in a deep breath, as if he had surfaced from a dive, feeling as if a hand had been gripping his throat.

Now wide awake, he felt sure he knew who the tall man was, angry that he was here in the mountains, and—he barely admitted to himself—afraid that number 76 had followed him. He squirmed from his sleeping bag and wriggled from the tiny tent. That was a feat in itself, one made more difficult by his irritation and not unlike the contortions of a very large moth twisting, turning, and finally bursting its cocoon.

Once on his feet, bootless and wearing only his underwear, Pitt—a near-naked, would-be champion in whatever fight ensued—stood before the entrance of the tent next to his, ready to pound the stranger, unaware that no one was in the tent.

"Help you with something?"

Pitt spun to face the speaker, spun so quickly he tripped on a rock and toppled on to the tent. He bounced back to his feet by sheer will power and, grabbing tent fabric and pole, realized all in one moment that he must look ridiculous. Josh sat on a large rock, calmly watching. He was a silhouette against the band of dark trees, but Pitt recognized his voice.

"Where's 76?" Pitt demanded, trying to steady his voice and regain a little composure.

"Who?"

"Number 76. Where is he?"

"I think you've got the wrong number. Want to try again?"

"The tall guy."

"You mean Lud?"

"Whatever! Where is he?"

"I don't know."

"What do you mean, you don't know?"

"He disappeared for a while. He does that sometimes."

Pitt stared into the darkness in Josh's direction and could think of nothing else to say, so he ambled back to his tent, angry and confused, yet trying to look steady and in control. For the rest of the night his mind switched between anxiety—because 76 or Lud or whoever he was, was out there somewhere—and rage, because he was not in control of the situation.

That night, for the first time, Pitt questioned his own sanity. Had he really, while nearly naked in the dark, confronted a man he barely knew? And had he done so because another man reminded him of a fight he had clearly lost?

Just after dawn he was building a fire to break the chill from the frosty, spring mountain air when the tall man walked into camp and nodded at Pitt, unaware of Pitt's eccentric display the night before. Lud gestured with his camera to the mountain peaks.

"Great photos of the sunrise on the mountains," he said as he stepped nearer the fire.

"Cold night to spend outside," Pitt deadpanned.

Lud snorted and crouched to warm his hands. They strained to make small talk, but words were scarce. Josh, now among them, made his own breakfast and packed up. Pitt did not ask where the others were going. He did not want to say where he was going, and he hoped Josh and 76—or whatever Josh had called him—would go in a different direction. But this was wishful thinking, and he knew it. Only one trail led deeper into the mountains, and all three men would take it.

Pitt still felt uncertain about the tall man. Lud—that was the name he recalled. He did not like him, did not trust him, was almost convinced this was the lanky forward who had made him—Pitt Cain, the man nobody pushed around, the one who would fight anything with fists, the player who could always change the game with pugnacity if not skill—look like an idiot.

That had hurt. He was a tough guy after all, a man's man, a man who could drink other men under the table, intimidate people, hang out with other tough guys, get to work on time no matter how bad the hangover, and seduce or at least force any woman he wanted to be with him, or so he liked to believe. And once on the job, he could carve dirt and knock down trees with the big dozer with precision and care, because he did care. He, the reckless perfectionist, cared about the work with his name on it, cared about how it looked to others, cared about how he treated the machine, yet cared nothing for his safety as he straddled sharp ledges and tempted gravity on steep slopes.

But something else rankled him deep down, and it bothered him now. The thing he expected to escape when he entered the mountains followed him, lived with him, nagged him. For a moment he missed Lor, missed her voice, because no matter how bad things were between them, something about her voice made him feel good. Even when she was telling him he was no good, he needed to hear that voice, because he admitted to himself now that she made him feel like something instead of nothing. Her large eyes told him, if he looked into them for long, that she was fascinated by his world, which she thought must be a better world than hers—hers a predictable island of limited choices, his a vast country of fascinating chances. And her eyes had convinced *him* this was true too. But not anymore.

For some of her words had dug a trench in Pitt's memory. "You're a drunk Pitt!" Maybe, he wondered, maybe he was just a drunk; maybe that was all. No, he was more than that. Tom had said so.

Pitt started up the trail, the day still new, the grass damp with dew, the air chilled. An eagle screeched a thousand feet above his head, and he felt the hair on his neck stand out, the chill of the air race up his spine, his greatest fear press on his lungs. Sirens and eagles both made him feel the same fear, and thinking about Lor made him feel even more lonely.

Feeling the need for comfort, he pulled his Scotch from his pack, poured it into the flask, and after gently replacing the bottle, took a drink. He felt the familiar comfort return. "That's better," he mumbled.

The other men were not yet on the trail, although he knew they would soon follow. But he did not know that still another would follow later, though farther back. And far ahead, an old bear sniffed the morning chill and clawed mounds of dirt away from a marmot's underground haven.

The peaks began closing in around the three hikers as they moved along the thin trail that looked like a fading scar on the shoulder of the mountain. On the right, spruce trees and boulders dotted the long scree slope, a remnant of a long-past avalanche; on the left, at the bottom of the slope, the river gurgled and splashed over the smooth rocks. The unlikely company of men trudged ahead.

"We've got to keep going upstream," Tom had told Pitt during his first trip into this country. At the memory of his old friend Pitt almost smiled, and he could not tell if he felt happy because of the contents of the flask or because Tom's words always seemed closer, current, comforting when he came back here. This, according to Tom, was still front country. "Takes time to get to God's country," he would say.

The trail took a sharp right turn around a sheer rock wall and then stopped abruptly as another slab of rock cut it off. But Pitt removed his pack, unsheathed the 44, and knelt down, disappearing into a tunnel at the base of the rock, a tunnel not easily seen by anyone who had not been there before. The others followed. Pitt remembered that he hated the claustrophobic tightness of the narrow passage, although Tom's presence and his encouragement would settle his mind. Not today. Suddenly he realized the others might be seeing him as the leader, the guide through new territory. The idea made the hole in the rock feel even smaller. Who, he wondered, was Josh? If he was a guide, if he knew the mountains, if he was taking Lud to high country to take pictures, had he been here before? Pitt would keep an eye on them both from now on, he decided; he would walk behind them.

Not a moment too soon for Pitt, he reached the opening and crawled out of the rock, pushing his pack and rifle ahead of him. He set down his pack and stretched but held his rifle in the crook of his arm. The other men emerged and leaned against the wall to rest. When all three were ready, Pitt said, "I'll follow behind." Josh assumed the lead, and they hiked along the mountain, gradually gaining elevation with the narrow trail. The valley widened but ended at a rock wall that rose fifteen hundred feet from the valley floor. The opposite end of the wall anchored a wide, almost square peak, one Pitt had scrambled up before after crossing the top of the wall—a massive, tilted mix of minerals and majesty pressed together by time and trouble.

The Majestic, as Tom had called it, dominated the valley like a watchman, effortlessly demanding attention. A waterfall leapt from a canyon in the wall near the place where it joined the Majestic, shooting out horizontally for several feet before beginning free-fall in dramatic form, tumbling, then roaring at the rocks below and bouncing back up a little before conforming to the canyon-like channel cut in the valley floor.

But the trail veered to the right of the dark rock wall and led travelers on a switchback journey over a brown shale col. The incline of the trail exhausted a man carrying a heavy pack, and Pitt was falling behind. After going back and forth across the face of the slope, he stopped and leaned back against the shale bank. He studied the trail all the way back to the place he had parked his truck, then looked out over the vast tree-covered hills until forest, sky, and his memories of what lay behind him merged into a hazy blue horizon.

He shut his eyes and listened to the rustle and roar of the falls, and he breathed slowly, trying to store the moment of peace, wondering if heaven were real, and if it were real, would it be like this? He hoped the place Tom had described would be peaceful, would fill the lonely tunnel that ran through Pitt's insides, would make sense of his life. He had never understood exactly what Tom meant as he'd hiked this trail with Pitt and talked about The Way, as he called it, or as he pointed to the rough, old cross hanging above the sink on the wall of his little house. Pitt wondered, as much as he wondered about anything, why the trail followed the path it did, and that question made him wonder why his life had turned out as it had.

During those times when Tom talked about life, Pitt learned that Tom had known Pitt's father and grandfather. "Your grandfather went through bad things at the school . . . bad things that made him mean and angry, and he used to take out his anger on Malen."

"What about you? You went away to the residential school, didn't you?" Pitt had asked.

"Yes, but things went better for me. I learned about The Way," Tom had said, as he pointed to the home-made cross. "Sister Grace taught me."

"Didn't my grandfather know the nun?"

"Sister Grace," Tom corrected. "Everybody knew her."

"Then why didn't she teach my grandpa?"

"She did. She taught everybody."

"Then why did Grandpa hate the school?"

Tom was quiet for moment. "Some things are hard to say."

"Like what?" Pitt had pressed.

"Not everybody was like Sister Grace. One man had authority over one of the boys' dorms, and he . . . he did things to some of the children."

"What things?"

"Things I cannot talk about."

"Why not?"

"They are too shameful . . . too horrible."

"And no one did anything?" Pitt's temper had begun to flare as he heard more.

"No one knew for a long time, and no one told because everybody who knew was scared."

"Scared of what?" Now Pitt's tone had become belligerent.

"Because the man who did those things told the boys he would tell their families what evil children they were and that something bad might happen to their families if they told."

"So he threatened them?"

"Yup. And your grandfather was hurt on the inside. Terribly hurt. He hated a lot because he hurt so much, and he taught your father to fear and to hate and to drink . . . lots."

Both men had been quiet for a while, news about his father's background swirling in Pitt's thoughts. Finally he asked, "Did you know my other grandfather?"

"Met him once, but didn't know him well. Seemed like a good man."

"Why did my old man hate him?"

"When Malen fell for your mother, he fell hard. They ran away. Got married. Lived in Pittsburgh for a while where Malen worked for a steel company. Didn't take long and he found out Amy's father was a preacher. He never forgave her for not telling him about her dad. He took it personally, and he would not allow her to see him again."

"But she did, didn't she?"

"Rumor is she saw him a couple of times."

"And she paid for it," Pitt had said, ending a conversation that had opened an old wound and a bad memory. Once, when his old man was drunk, Pitt had heard him talk about Pittsburgh. Malen had babbled on about the steel mill, the city, and how he had named Pitt for Pittsburgh. "Best times of my life," he had said before he fell asleep in his chair.

Pitt shook his head and opened his eyes, drifting back to the present. Back down the valley, he thought he saw movement along the trail. A bear? No, it looked like a man—a man standing stock still. Pitt fumbled with a side pocket of his pack, pulled out hefty, old binoculars, and hoisted them to his eyes. But he could not find the man. Great, he thought. The country was getting too crowded. He pulled out his flask and quenched his thirst. "No wonder this pack's so heavy," he muttered as he stuffed the flask and the binoculars into it.

"You all right down there?" the voice from the next switchback above called down. It was Josh. Pitt ignored him, sighed, and trudged up the trail. He was surprised at how well Josh kept up the pace and how confident he was on the trail. In places where the trail was faint, game trails braided with it, and one could easily take the wrong path. But Josh moved effortlessly, and he was cheerful, and that bothered Pitt, who felt neither happy nor fit.

The third man, however, was not so fit. Lud, the one Pitt was more sure with each passing hour had squared off with him at center ice, seemed to be sick and struggling—Lud the lanky man trying to keep up to Josh, the man Pitt did not trust. Put a helmet on a man and a guy could tell who he was. Pitt had heard him gagging and vomiting in the willows along the trail before they reached the tunnel. He was slowing Josh down, a fact that pleased Pitt but seemed to have no effect on Josh, who hiked along as if on a mission.

Pitt had hoped the others would move farther ahead as he plodded along behind them. He wanted a quiet camp away from them and away from whomever was far down the valley behind him. Their company was unwelcome.

He caught up with Josh and Lud at a clearing where he had camped before, one situated logically for hikers who would typically cover almost fifteen miles over rough terrain after leaving the last campsite. They set up camp in silence, a quiet imposed by fatigue but with a quickness required by their hunger.

Lud rose from driving a tent peg into the ground, tripped on the cord held by the peg, and tumbled into Pitt, knocking the shorter, stockier man back. Pitt, with his lower center of gravity, recovered quickly and grabbed instinctively, even eagerly for Lud, clutched his shirt with his left hand, and drew back his right before the other man could regain his balance. As seconds go, these ones were long, delicious, opportunity-filled moments when the other man, a man Pitt wanted to hate, was off balance. But before Pitt could follow through, Josh, with strength that seemed out of proportion with his slight build, grabbed Pitt's forearm.

Pitt looked into Josh's eyes and saw something he did not understand, yet something he wished for himself. A less self-centered man, a man more aware of human subtleties, a man less distracted by his desire for the next drink might have recognized the look in those eyes, might have identified it not as anger, not as fear, but as justice—the certainty that one has the right to defend something he believes to be deep and right and good. Pitt released Lud's shirt, pushing him away and jerking free of Josh's vice-like grip at the same time.

"What's wrong with you? Do you know who I am?" he demanded.

"Do *you* know who you are?" Josh answered evenly, not flinching or backing away.

"Well, what's wrong with him?" Pitt asked, gesturing toward Lud, who was walking away, leaving the camp.

"He's got his demons too," Josh said.

"Next time you step into my business, you'll be sorry. What's-his-name doesn't need your help."

"I wasn't helping him, Pitt. I was helping you." Josh's calm expression, the soft certainty of his words, the bright intensity of his eyes left Pitt frustrated and confused.

CHAPTER NINE

The next morning, Lud was sitting by the fire when Pitt crawled from his tent, jammed his boots on, and proceeded to untie the rope that suspended his food bag in a tree. Although bleary-eyed, he was wary about the man at the fire and had noticed that the third tent's flap was open. No one was inside. So they were alone—just Pitt and 76, for now he felt certain that Lud and number 76 were one and the same. Good things happen to those who wait, he thought to himself. Wasn't that somewhere in the Bible? He didn't care about the source of the idea; the saying made him feel good for a moment. But his head hurt; his whisky was gone; his attitude had soured. Back at the fire, he mixed some dough and wrapped it on a stick, then held it over the fire.

"How long you play for the Green Machine?" Pitt asked.

Lud looked up from the big, blue book he was reading and looked at Pitt, his eyes glancing side to side. "Couple months," he said hesitantly.

"Where you from?"

"Toronto."

"Where'd you play?"

"Princeton. Played college hockey there for a while. Had a scholarship."

"How come you left?" Pitt asked, looking for the story behind the only man—a man too young—to best him in a scrap on skates.

"Some trouble."

Pitt accepted this as enough information for now. A citizen of a small town where folks were given to talk too much about people and things they knew nothing about, he thought he had pushed as far as he could. He would circle around and find another way.

"How come you're out here?"

"Josh invited me."

"He from Princeton too?"

Lud did not answer. Pitt heard footsteps, then saw Josh entering the clearing from the way they had traveled the day before.

"See anyone else down the trail?" Pitt changed the subject.

"Nobody."

Pitt poured a cup of coffee from the pot on the fire. Campfire coffee was strong, hot, and unsophisticated, untouched by a barista, not flavored with syrup, uncut with cream. He sipped it between bites of the hot biscuit on the end of the stick, and his head felt slightly better.

"I need a drink," he blurted.

"Maybe you need this," Lud said as he extended the blue book.

Pitt waved his hand. "Keep your goody-goody book. I don't need it." Having learned a little about Lud, he decided to question Josh. "Where'd you get a name like Josh?" he asked bluntly.

"My father gave it to me." Where did your name come from?"

"My old man named me."

"But why 'Pitt'?"

"Named for Pittsburgh, where he worked for a while."

"Do they live in Emerald Lake?"

"No. My mother's in heaven. My old man should be in hell, if you believe in that stuff."

"Any other family around? Of course I've met Gracie."

"Nah. Not besides her. My mother's father might be around still. I don't know."

Pitt thought about his grandfather. He was a no-good preacher, according to Pitt's old man. Pitt had grown up hating his mother's dad, although he had met him only once long ago when, as a small boy, he went with his mother to the train station. There he had met a dignified middle-aged man, well-dressed and well-spoken even to the ears of a six-year-old, and with kind eyes that listened to young Pitt without moving away to look around at other more important things the way most grown-ups' eyes did.

The next day, Pitt had found his mother sobbing, head buried in her hands, body shaking, crying from deep inside, unaware her young son was watching and listening. She had jolted upright and moved quickly away when he touched her. Then, seeing Pitt, just as quickly as she had moved away she crouched down and held him closely, but not before he had seen her black eyes. She had fallen, she said. He had known even then that this was her way of protecting him from the truth. Malen had forbidden contact with her father and had flown into a rage when he found out about the meeting at the train station. As Pitt's mind wandered from the memories of his mother, he looked back at Josh, who was watching him and smoking a big cigar.

"Why are you smoking that thing?" Pitt asked. He had a bad memory of stealing one of his old man's Cubans and smoking it down to the end, then feeling dizzy, then nauseated, then hurling the contents of his stomach again and again in the bushes behind the old house. He shuddered as he remembered the taste of regurgitated nicotine.

"To celebrate," Josh answered. "Actually, the cigar is smoking. I'm just pulling air through the tobacco, then blowing smoke out my mouth. Can you believe people actually inhale this stuff? But I like the smell."

"Celebrate what?"

"Everything that's beautiful and good. But," he added, "I celebrate in moderation."

Then he smiled at Pitt and tapped out the cigar.

"I pegged you as a goody-goody. I mean, you're stinkin' the place up."

"It's a Cuban. Want one?"

"No! I quit cigars. And aren't those illegal?"

"Not where I come from. Now who's the goody-goody? Anyway—your choice. But we ought to enjoy the things we make, don't you think? I never inhale though. I just love the aroma."

"Whatever, man."

Lud accepted the cigar Josh offered and began smoking it eagerly. It was still early, and the air was heavy, the sky dulled by grey-blue clouds, so low they were almost within reach, and as the men packed their camp, the rain suddenly fell hard, soaking the surface of everything in seconds. They struggled hurriedly into rain gear, hoisted their packs, and started walking. Lightning made taking shelter under a tree a bad idea. The tents were already packed, and they had no other shelter. So they walked up the path that, within minutes, became a creek that flooded their boots and drowned their socks as they slogged and slipped and tripped to still higher ground.

Then the hail began—a few small stones at first, then a wall of white, blasting over the ridge on their right, raking their faces, forcing their eyes shut like a million needles flung with skill, drawn from some violent, malevolent force, at once powerful, careless, and oblivious to the pain of the men leaning forward with their heads bowed to the fury of the storm. Their feet fought gravity and tried to gain ground, to outlast the storm that assaulted their senses, slowed their gait to a crawl, and curtained their world in white.

Pitt heard someone singing, or at least he thought he did. But the roar of the hail sounded as though a train was charging past them, threatening to grind them into the rocks in the valley below. Still, through the deafening, thundering boom of the ice, he heard shreds of music, indistinct but calming.

As quickly as it began, the storm subsided. Pitt still heard music and realized that Josh was softly singing a tune that was both familiar and far away, a song Pitt felt he knew yet could not sing. Where had he heard it?

The hikers came around a bend in the trail and stopped. The storm had poured so much water on the mountains that a gully had become a torrent, roaring down the mountain, carrying debris and rocks the size of a man's head. The water was running almost two feet deep and eight feet wide. Across the valley, they could see other rivers running down the gullies, collecting water and channeling it to the widening river below.

"Lousy place to spend the night," Lud said, as he surveyed their options.

"We'll have to wait for it to settle down," Pitt shouted above the racket of the water, and he leaned against the rocky slope.

"Maybe not," Josh yelled.

He tied a rope around his waist and handed the other end to Pitt. Then he picked up a rock, large and heavy enough that he had to stoop to hold it while cradling it against his thighs. The rock would give him stability against the force of the water. Pitt thought Josh was either brave or crazy or maybe both, but he instinctively grabbed the rope, ready to reel in the slight, wiry man if he lost his footing.

Taking small, shuffling steps to keep the rush of water from sweeping his feet off the remainder of the trail and moving somewhat like a penguin, Josh inched his way to the other side of the current where he sat down facing the other men, holding the rope taut, and beckoning them to follow. Lud's expression revealed his doubt.

"Is he serious?"

Pitt nodded and gestured for Lud to go ahead. Holding the rope and crouching low, Lud pulled himself hand over hand through the torrent of water, looking like a man shriveled with arthritis. Pitt admitted to himself that he enjoyed watching lanky 76 struggle against the force of the water. And as Pitt held his end of the rope and watched, he considered letting the rope slacken, just for a moment, to see what would happen. But he thought better of it, while he grinned at the ground, imagining a frightened, tall, slightly clumsy man reacting to the loosened tension.

Finally, it was Pitt's turn. He tied the rope around his waist, set his thick thighs into a tuck position and started wading across the muddy spout of water and silt. Just over halfway across, he became more confident. He lifted his foot to stride rather than scrape the sole of his boot along the rock base. The force of the water drove his left foot over the edge at the same time as a stone the size of a child's fist smashed the face of his wrist watch. He yelped, more from surprise than pain, but the combination of the stone's impact and his loose footing tipped his weight too near the edge. He fell flat on the trail in an attempt not to go over the edge. But he was submerged and going over, and he felt the rope's slackness, and he doubted the others could hold him. In fact, he doubted they would risk trying.

In one second, he fell from control to panic. His head under the freezing water, his right elbow the only limb giving him leverage on the rock, he braced for a fall and gripped the rope tightly, just as he felt someone seize the shoulder straps on his pack and heave him toward the safety of the other side. Gasping, he landed on top of his rescuer before struggling to his feet and stumbling a few steps until he could lean against the trail. He was soaked, chilled, and humiliated, the way men sometimes feel when they lose their footing, when they need to rely on someone else's strength, when they cannot succeed alone.

Later that evening, in dry clothes and with a full stomach, Pitt looked up at the clear sky, a sky that had threatened him hours earlier, now a canopy of deepening blue—the expanse. It was late. And in the northern nighttime summer air, if one waits long enough, the stars reveal themselves, timidly at first, like wedding night lovers self-consciously showing themselves in the dark. Arcturus, then the summer triangle of Vega, Deneb, and Altair appear, faintly at first, gradually growing brighter and brighter as their neighbors appear, forming the ancient pictures of Lyra, the Northern Cross, and Aquila, The Eagle.

"That was some day," Lud said to no one in particular, as he stared into the glow of the fire, a glow that skipped across their faces and back again.

"Sometimes the best journeys start out the worst," Josh said.

After that, no one said anything. All three were exhausted and quiet. But Pitt looked across the flames at Josh, and, although he still resented the man's presence, he felt he had to say something, but to thank him would be to drop his guard, to give up his distance, to surrender a little control. Still, he wondered how a man that much lighter than he was could have hoisted him up and out of danger. He stood. The others paid no attention. He looked at Josh for a moment. Then he walked away into the deepening darkness. He was curious about something.

CHAPTER TEN

Back down the trail, Pitt found what he was looking for. He had learned from Tom how to slip quietly through the brush, how to avoid stepping on sticks that might snap, and how to step lightly, no small feat for a man of 250 pounds. Once he was far enough away from his own camp fire, his skills had enabled him to follow the aroma of other smoke until he saw a faint glow reflected against a rock. He had been curious about the man he had seen from the ridge by The Majestic, and he had wondered, since Josh and Lud had seen another truck at the trailhead, why they had not seen another backpacker before they caught up with him at the first night's camp.

Pitt could not be sure, but he thought he knew the man who sat back from the fire. He was obviously a man with some back country experience. His small fire was built so that its heat would reflect against the rock wall. Pitt watched quietly from well back in the shadow of a timorous, lonely spruce tree that had managed somehow to reach higher than the surrounding patches of brush. The tree's height did not imply its age. This was high country on the upper edge of the tree line, where a small tree might take decades of short growing seasons to become even minimal cover for people or predators . . . or both. Pitt and Tom had passed the little old tree several times on trips into this area.

The man at the fire leaned forward to set another stick in the flames, and Pitt could see his profile for the first time. Now he was almost certain he knew the stranger's identity. Almost. If he was correct, why would this one be camped out in the wilderness? And was he keeping his distance from Pitt and the others on purpose?

It was time to leave, and as Pitt pressed his hand to the ground behind him, his weight cracked a twig he did not feel before it snapped. The camper's head jerked in his direction, wary and watching. But, knowing the man would be partially blind from the light of the fire, Pitt kept still and quiet. Finally, when the startled man seemed satisfied that he was alone, he turned away. But Pitt took nothing for granted and, keeping the spruce tree between himself and the man's camp, he barely breathed as he inched back into the blackening silence of the night.

The man was experienced, as Pitt had observed. Moreover, Pitt had guessed correctly that he knew him. Leaning against a boulder cast there by some unknown, unrecorded event in another century, the strange man waited, believing time was on his side, considering each potential move, anticipating finishing what he had started long ago, certain that the forces to which he had committed his life were strong.

The stranger was familiar with Pitt, had been familiar with him for a long time. But he had been away from this part of the country, traveling and settling in a town, then moving and shifting identities again, never staying in one place more than a few years, never letting anyone know him well, always manipulating everyone to his advantage while pretending to have their best interests at heart, feigning good intentions, departing before the good will ran out, and leaving behind as much turmoil as he could. He was good at evil.

In one small city, he had quickly become popular with the inner circle who knew the right people, had gotten himself elected to city council, influenced the hiring of the maintenance department head, then lobbied for the purchase of heavy equipment from a company owned by his brother, who paid him a good cut for his efforts. When news of some irregularities in the acquisitions began to surface, he knew nothing of any wrong doing, and pointed to the department head, saying that he had been concerned about hiring the man in the first place. As all eyes focused on the sacrificial lamb in the department, the councilor humbly announced his resignation, citing personal reasons. He quickly left town, and was never heard from again.

Having satisfied a little of his political appetite, he arrived at the next place as the new owner of a failing internet café. He enhanced the décor with bongs and various drug paraphernalia for sale. Customers could also secretly purchase hallucinogens, addictive drugs that hurt the hungry, the mentally ill, and the naïve. His new address was far enough across the country that nobody recognized the name of the former regional politician. Only his partners knew where he had gone, and they kept their distance. They offered just enough cash to help him get started, but they would have denied any knowledge of his existence or his agenda, which was to infiltrate and destabilize institutions and communities, a plan designed to make people suspicious of leaders and resentful of organizations.

He was good at what he did. In the prairie town, he generously made himself available to the local business organization, and because its board was always short of volunteers, he quickly became an executive member. Good with words, smart with numbers, he devised a plan that would put the community on the map as a destination. People would come from across the nation and beyond to see the local sand hills, hunt antelope and deer, and fish in the new trout ponds. Of course, he had contacts that would help establish the thriving, local tourism industry, and for a fee, he could coordinate everything.

But he had no such contacts, and he signed no real contracts. The papers he presented at council meetings and endless meetings of the business group were fakes with phony signatures, while his fee was conveniently stuffed into his savings account under the name of a numbered company in the bank in another city. He was getting tired of moving around, even though he still loved the adrenaline rush of living on the edge, baiting the trap, and moving in for the kill.

However, after two years in the prairie town with no sign of more tourists and no new development, the mayor—a retired cop who got into politics because he wanted to keep busy and who was a cynic who suspected anyone new of being up to no good—started asking too many questions. Overnight, the internet café closed and its owner disappeared.

The stranger had been in Emerald twice before, briefly and years earlier, but he had traveled with a different crowd then, and no one remembered him. In fact he had expended significant effort in order to ensure that no one would recognize him. A month after leaving the prairie town, he appeared in Emerald, sporting a new name and a closely cropped haircut, having shorn off his graying ponytail and beard. As a result, he appeared monk-like, and his wardrobe of simple brown or black augmented this image. His new name, for the time being, was Harvey Trudeau.

But the image, as all his facades had been, was phony. Within a year after arriving in the mountain town, he was elected to the deacons' board of the little, storefront church, he being the perfect prayer partner for the young pastor, who expressed appreciation for the new deacon's devotion. Dispensing wisdom to the struggling disciple, offering comfort to the lonely grandmother, or saying "Amen," at a quiet moment in the sermon—all these Brother Harvey performed with quiet dignity, showing empathy, sharing his own stories of spiritual growth, which, though fictitious, resonated in the sincere hearts of the gullible, if not all the faithful.

All this he was able to do while watching Pitt Cain, listening to conversations in the coffee shop, and asking questions—the kind of queries that stayed in people's minds because they were actually statements, more like accusations.

"What had ever happened," he wondered out loud, "in the case of old Tom?" "Why," he pondered, "had no one ever been prosecuted for Tom's death?" Trudeau had heard about the story in the news some years ago. His questions were met with uncomfortable shifts in posture and side-long glances. No one wanted to talk about the topic because everyone, at least almost everyone, wanted to believe the case had been forgotten, if not solved.

So the stranger continued sowing seeds of discontent where he could, not only in the community but also in the little group of worshipers with whom he had associated himself. Someone had a problem with the pastor? Brother Harv would offer a sympathetic ear, smile knowingly, and say little, yet enough to signal that he too had concerns about young pastor Mike. A couple of senior members of the congregation confided to the deacon that they wished he were their pastor. He began leading a Bible study for them that had nothing to do with the Bible but everything to do with an investment opportunity for people of faith like them. He was the perfect church bully. No one knew what he was up to—no one except the member who had seen the deacon's kind before, and she kept her distance. Gracie Cain was nobody's fool. And there was a new fellow with a dark complexion—a Josh somebody—who bothered Trudeau, because no matter how sweetly he spoke to the newcomer, Josh, the deacon could not learn anything useful about him.

Then Pitt's fight with number 76 had spilled into the gossip at the Mountain View Café, and rumors surfaced, saying that he had pulled a gun on Switz, the attorney who had shacked up with his Pitt's ex. The stranger watched and listened. And when Pitt left his cabin and drove off into the mountains, the watcher knew the time had come, as it always did, to make a killing, only this time the pay-off was not monetary or part of the disruptive plans of the secret society to which he had committed his soul. This time it was personal. Three hours after Pitt had left the cabin, the stranger had followed, allowing time for the younger man to get ahead and out of sight, taking time to think through his next moves, enjoying visions of the moment when he would get some justice.

Harvey Trudeau's plans had become complicated when Josh, the new fellow with the dark, unreadable eyes, came up the trail with a gangly companion in tow. But the erstwhile deacon was patient, because he always got his way.

A few minutes after watching the stranger's camp, Pitt was back in his own tent, and after the necessary contortions, he was in his sleeping bag. Worries lingered in his imagination about the man he had spied on down the trail, but fear of what lay ahead soon replaced them. He had been so frustrated with his unwanted company and preoccupied with the man following them that he had forgotten about his destination—the place Tom told him about, a place of healing, hidden beauty, fullness. From now on, he decided, he would keep his mind on that goal. And he drifted off to sleep, and he dreamed.

In his dream, he heard a voice, barely a whisper, more of a breath, telling him what to do. "Pick up the stone," he heard the voice say, but he ignored the urging, which was as much a feeling as a word. After taking a few more steps, he heard another sound—a grunting just off the trail to his right, and he thought he saw movement through the dense, low growth in the forest. Then silence. He walked ahead, his legs heavy, his pack enormous and awkward, the big book in his hand making him feel clumsy as he reached for his rifle, but it was missing from the scabbard. Then the black bear emerged from the trees and stood on its back legs on the trail ahead. The bear was enormous; others joined it, smaller bears, filling the trail and blocking the way ahead. He was frozen with fear. He looked at his hands. They were pale and small, and they held only the big book. It was a Bible. He tried to drop it and run, but it clung to his hands, and he could not move. Then Josh came by, whistling the same tune he had sung in the hail storm. Calmly he tossed a stone at the biggest bear, who ambled with the others up the trail and disappeared. Pitt woke up. Josh was at the campfire, whistling. It was morning, and the coffee brewing on the fire smelled like redemption from his nightmare.

CHAPTER ELEVEN

For the second time on this trip, Pitt wondered if he might be going crazy, if he had snapped under the pressure of life, of losing Lor, of losing control of his life. He could not allow himself to think about that. This was it, he decided, the day he would forget about the past and start over.

After a quick breakfast, Pitt found himself alone, staring at the remains of the dying fire. He noticed that the others were packed and starting up the trail, realized he was in no hurry to hit the trail again, and thought of spending the day in camp, letting Josh and Lud get a day ahead of him. Finally, he could be by himself. But the feelings in his dream of the night before, if not the dream itself, still simmered. Like a fragrance after a woman walks by, his nightmare still kept drawing his attention, intruding on his logic, motivating his movements. So he tossed the last of his coffee on the embers, packed and hiked on, still able to see the other men as they ascended toward another ridge.

Around noon he stopped and ate some beef jerky, enjoying the silence of the sunny day. He had watched his back trail, yet had seen no sign of the stranger. But more consistently, he had kept Josh and Lud in sight, not wanting to catch them, not willing to be alone, not wanting them to think he needed them. He knew where they were—above him on switchbacks that would top out at eleven thousand feet, then descend into a valley on the other side of the ridge.

An eagle screeched high overhead, and the hair on the back of his neck stood up as a shiver ran down either side of his spine. The sound always got to him in the same way sirens did. Maybe, he admitted, both made him feel that trouble was on its way or that he was in the wrong place. He hated the sound.

At the highest point of the pass, he caught up to the others. The last few hundred feet of the trail had been covered with snow. And now they had entered the ice fields. It seemed as if they had ascended into a different universe, brilliant white, yet etched or dusted in shades of browns. Great grey rock sentinels were in random places, like crouching gargoyles, guarding the ice field, silent, forbidding, formal. A chunk of ice the size of Pitt's truck broke away from the glacier that was hanging from the ledge of the mountain. The break sounded like cannon fire, and the ice crackled, then roared, then echoed as it splintered down the slope and poured itself into a gigantic snow cone at the foot of the glacier that it had fallen from.

Pitt leaned against a large rock and pulled on his crampons, aware that the snowy slope could have patches of hard ice, knowing that a careless step would send a man sliding and more than likely tumbling to the bottom. Josh had already attached the same claw-like devices to the bottoms of his boots. Pitt watched him, observed that his eyes were closed, as though he were praying or meditating, as if he were absent from his body. He seemed different now from when Pitt had first met him in Gracie's cramped office. He looked older, more serious, maybe even troubled. Josh sat that way, unmoving for twenty minutes, while Pitt grew impatient. Just when he decided to descend into the valley alone, Josh appeared to be ready.

They stood, looking northwest on the edge of the valley, a valley so deep that the trees in the bottom looked like a dark carpet and not like trees at all. Pitt had traveled this dim valley before, and he shivered involuntarily as he gazed into its black depths. In every other direction, walls of ice suspended precariously from ragged ledges that clung to high peaks, the pass over which they had climbed being the only break in the spectacular cathedral of time-and-storm-chiseled giants.

"This is where we go down," Pitt said, pointing to a small break in the rocks that ringed the upper lip of the valley like a parapet on the wall of a castle.

"Doesn't look like a trail to me," Lud said warily. He was talking to himself, but his words rankled Pitt just the same.

"Find another way then, college boy," Pitt said, and he was over the ledge and out of sight before anyone could answer. He was feeling the strength of the mountains now, and he was locked on to his destination, the place Tom had described but that Pitt had not seen. The mountains could make a man feel afraid, but they can also make him feel invincible, large, and free—as though he can do anything, whether or not he has the skills. Pitt had seen this recklessness in Lud, who refused to strap on the crampons Josh had offered.

Josh had listened as Pitt and Lud had a heated argument about crampons, a sparring match that ended with Pitt saying, "You're a moron, 76, and don't expect me to drag your busted head out of here when you crash."

"It won't be my head getting busted!" Lud had retorted. Josh had stepped between them.

"The trail, gentlemen," he had said, gesturing toward the valley.

The trail, having become thread-like at best, ended. From now on they would navigate by memory and when necessary by compass. Snow was still clinging to the steep scree, and they turned right, traversing the slope at an angle that led them down. The sun had baked a crust on to the surface of the enormous mountain-side slab of snow, and the crust shattered under the weight of their steps with the result that their steps sank to mid-calf and deeper.

So began their descent into the valley. Josh remarked that it reminded him of Gehenna. When Pitt and Lud looked at each other and Pitt shrugged, Josh explained that this was a valley outside ancient Jerusalem, a valley that had been a smoldering, stinking garbage dump and a metaphor of hell. But in the mountain gorge they were walking into, the larch trees were lush and the valley floor appeared more and more brilliant green as they drew nearer. Still, they were well above the tree line and a hundred feet from the lower edge of the snow field.

They stopped at a wide, mountain-side cascade that ran steep and cold, deep and fast. The water rumbled from an outcropping of rock a hundred feet above, then disappeared underground just above them. They stood still then, the group of three, while the boisterous stream hushed everything around and within them. Even their thoughts were quieted by the sound that overwhelmed the self-importance of analysis. They stood there, having developed an uneasy alliance, three unforeseen partners, each on his own quest, two of them on a journey they thought was a secret, one on a mission the others could not comprehend.

A few steps away from the falls, the ice on the trail had a harder surface. "So, what are you—a Baptist, Jewish, or what?" Pitt asked Josh, naming all of the religious groups from his limited mental catalogue of such things.

"I think of myself as a shepherd," Josh answered with no further explanation. Pitt noticed Josh's hands. They looked old, much older than the man himself; they looked gnarled, and they looked scarred, but strong. Josh was a hard man to figure out, Pitt thought.

Suddenly, Lud was flailing, tumbling, and sliding down the icy slope before his terrified shriek shredded the idyllic tones of the waterfall behind them. His companions turned around, carefully maintaining their own footing, and watched as the unforgiving gravity and slick surface of the slope slid the gangly man down with remarkable speed. His arms and legs and hiking poles flailed to no effect until a huge rock, jutting up through the ice and snow stopped his descent abruptly, his head hitting the rock with a "clunk." Josh was confidently jamming his crampons into the snow, making his way down to help the unconscious hiker before Pitt was able to set aside his disgust for Lud, who had refused to wear the right equipment.

"Moron," he grunted, and started toward the limp form.

"He's alive." Josh had found a pulse by the time Pitt had crept down the slope. Lud stirred, then scrambled to his feet, looked at the others, and collapsed again.

"Where's my camera?" he demanded.

"Likely in your pack?" Pitt answered.

"No! It was right here!" Lud patted his chest where he thought the expensive camera should be.

"Great. He's delirious," Pitt said to Josh. Then, more quietly, "Moron."

Josh shot a withering glance at Pitt, and handed a pair of crampons to Lud, who frowned stupidly and fumbled with them until Josh knelt and attached them to his boots. "We've got to get down from here and make camp," Josh said. "Pitt, lead the way and find a safe way for us to get down."

"Find it yourself," Pitt answered. He was exasperated, and he wanted out. He wanted to hike alone, find the ancient lake, start again, and leave behind both the mystery of a man who called himself a shepherd and the babbling, concussed moron who was struggling to string words into a sentence.

He turned and stamped his feet, step after careful step into the icy mountain, but not before seeing the look in Josh's eyes. Was it anger or deep sadness? Whatever it was, the look left Pitt feeling remorse as he walked away, hoping to be alone, yet becoming lonely and more fearful as the memories of this place returned and the darkness of the forest drew closer.

He stepped into the trees, the first of which had grown only to shoulder height, but in some places they grew like solid walls lining a hallway, their deep green dimming the bright sun. He found a game trail that angled down the slope. Pitt followed it through taller trees that led into an open meadow colored with masses of small flowers already jumping to life, knowing somehow that the growing season was short, gathering in light from the long days.

He smelled something foul and instantly knew he was not alone. Sliding the 44 from its sheath, he quickly surveyed the meadow and thought he saw something moving into the forest on the opposite side, but he could not be sure. The old she-bear was around. He was sure. He could smell her, for a bear can stink like a garbage dump.

He blamed the bear for Tom's death, and he blamed the bear for what happened between him and Lor. He hated the old sow, and he admitted to himself that this trip was not only about healing, but also about hunting revenge. About killing the thing that had killed him, as though he could destroy the memories and wipe out the past, as if a single shot had the power to end his trouble and his rage. Seeing no more sign of trouble, he kept his rifle in hand, just to be safe. If she were hunting him, good! "Bring it on, old stink," he muttered.

Continuing on, Pitt recognized silverberry and buffalo berry shrubs, both with edible, though unappealing, berries. But the star of the meadow was the yellow glacier lily that grew profusely. In places, it grew where snow still lay crusted and glistening.

Using his fingers, he dug a few lily bulbs out of the dirt.

Twenty minutes later, walking on a fallen tree that reached from bank to bank, he crossed the river on the valley floor. Finding a deep pool, he carefully cast a fly to the surface of the cold, dark water. The fly, one he had tied himself, bobbed on ripples created out of the passing current and began drifting downstream. A second before the fly entered the white water, a splash in the current, a jerk on the fly rod, a dance to the surface of the pool, and a small trout was hooked. Pitt smiled and reeled in the valiantly fighting fish, removed the hook, and after bashing the fish's head against a rock, tossed it a little way up the bank before casting the fly back on the water. A second, then a third fish bit, the last being bigger than the others. They were small, but they would be a fresh, welcome change from the dried fruit and dehydrated meals of the past few days. He had expected to travel alone and more quickly. He had nearly run out of food.

The ridges high above the valley were already blocking the sun, making the low ground cool and the light dim. He knew he needed to find a place to camp, but he kept checking his back trail, kept thinking he could smell the old bear, wondering if she was hunting him, imagining that she remembered him. The small clearing he had camped at before was close, and he quickened his pace, driven by sudden hunger and not a little bit of fear.

The sound he heard was not the grunt of a bear but a human voice. His relief was replaced by irritation when he recognized the whining tones of Lud, who looked up as Pitt entered the small clearing. A fire crackled in the center. Lud grinned, tried to stand, and crumbled to the ground, tumbling sideways, clumsily grabbing Josh by the shoulder. Josh, seeming oblivious to Lud, smiled at Pitt.

"Make yourself at home," he said.

Pitt was perplexed that the other hikers were already in camp, especially when Josh had been supporting Lud's gangly frame in what must have been an awkward trek from the slope to the camp. But no one offered any explanation, and Pitt acted as though he did not care. In the slight breeze, he sniffed another hint of the she-bear he feared was too close, but he went about setting up camp. He noticed Josh watching him, and the attention bothered him, because he hated being watched, disliked the close quarters, and resented these intruders in his space. At the same time, Pitt admitted that he did not mind their company on this evening at least, found a little comfort in their proximity, and supposed he could be sharing the clearing with worse.

He cooked the lily bulbs and the fish, but he ate only two of the bulbs. Too many could make him vomit; this he knew from the first time he had eaten them, had ignored Tom's caution, and had wretched in the tall grass until his stomach felt beyond empty as Tom sat chuckling by the campfire.

He could use a talk with Tom right now, and the memory of the old man filled him with a sadness he felt too tired to shake. But Lud had been babbling some nonsense about flying from the rock to the campsite, saying he could not have made it without the helicopter.

"I didn't hear any chopper," Pitt said, realizing as he said it that Lud was still quite concussed and less than rational. Still, Pitt wondered how the two men got to the clearing ahead of him. He peered through the trees to what little he could see of the snowy saddle on the mountain.

"Well, we nearly made it didn't we, Jim?" Lud was speaking again and looking at Pitt, waiting for an answer.

"You mean Pitt. Nearly made what?"

"The team man. The team!" Lud answered. He looked over at Josh, who was looking into the trees with his back to the fire. Then in a low voice, as if he had a secret to tell Pitt, Lud continued, "And you know why we didn't make it? We got bumped by the coach's kid and his buddy. That's why. Man, my head hurts." He leaned back against a tree, closed his eyes, and within a minute began snoring.

Josh, who sat motionless and looked dead tired, had turned to face the fire. It was smoking, smothered and useless. He separated two pieces of wood, and flames leapt between them, the fire licking the sides, then the top, as though it were a desert dog to which someone offered water—tentative at first, then as it gained strength more eager, then insatiable and careless. Sap in one piece of wood exploded and spewed sparks into the air, throwing a glowing ember onto Lud's pants, waking him up and causing him to jump to his feet and brush away the burning chunk. Pitt and Josh both chuckled at him, and he sat down again, holding his head.

"Relationships are like fire," Josh said. Pitt rolled his eyes.

Lud interjected, "One burning coal can't survive on its own."

"That's not what I meant. Two pieces of wood too close together can't benefit each other. The fire needs space for oxygen; friends need to let each other breath too, or they smother each other."

"Hm," Pitt grunted involuntarily. "Sounds like my marriage." Before he knew it, he was spewing details. "I wanted space, and she wanted me . . . all the time, it seemed like. But we did produce a lot of sparks."

"Sounds like the woman in your mind was different from the woman in your marriage."

"What's that supposed to mean?"

"You loved a fantasy, but you lived with a female—a real human being."

What Pitt did not admit was that he missed her now, and sadness, like the grief he had felt for Tom, returned. Josh was still listening, as if hearing what Pitt was not saying, as if knowing something needed saying, as if in the saying of the right words something might happen—not an action or a miracle but some kind of cleansing. But Pitt had said more than he intended, and he stood and walked into the trees.

A thought stirred, a thought he had suppressed, an idea as wild and unlikely as this deep valley, an idea only feasible in this place, hidden as it was from his realities, a story that suggested he might fix things with Lor. "Nah," he said out loud, stuffing the plot back inside the cover of an imaginary story he dared not read. "Who are you kidding?" he muttered, rebuking himself. But maybe, he thought. Maybe he could be the man she needed him to be. Maybe she could forgive him. He imagined himself serving Lor and treating her well, as he had not done for a long time—probably never, he admitted to himself. Maybe when he went back, maybe he would have another chance. What had happened between them? Too much. And now there was Switz, and how he fit in the story was more than Pitt wanted to think about.

On the way back to the fire, he was startled by a stumbling Lud who had also walked into the bush to relieve himself. "Man, I'm not built for the backcountry," he whined.

Ignoring him, Pitt sat down again on the patch of earth he had occupied before. As he did, he smelled the stink of the old she-bear again. He looked across the fire at Josh who was looking back at him. Each man saw in the other's eyes a mutual awareness of the presence of the bear. But Pitt saw something else in Josh's look that he had seen before but could not identify, knowledge beyond Pitt's comprehension, a concern older than his years, a discerning perhaps, deeper than one could easily understand. He had wondered often what made this new resident of Emerald tick, and he decided that now was the time to ask.

"Just one more thing I want to say Pitt," Josh said, as he built up the fire. "Hope is easy for a man to give up on."

"Hope! Is this a Sunday School lesson? Do you know who I am—things I've done?"

"Do *you* know who you are? That's the bigger question."

Pitt felt the question as much as he heard it, and he disliked the feeling, disliked the man who asked, disliked that he could not fish out a smart-sounding comeback from any reservoir in his imagination. This was one of those questions that made a man think, and if he does not want to think and does not want to figure, he just feels mad. He reached for the flask and, finding it absent from his shirt pocket, sat still and stared into the fire, as though he might find himself there, as though inspiration might emerge, genie-like, from the smoke, revealing something that might fill what he was beginning to recognize as a dark tunnel as long as his memories and as empty as his dreams had become.

"Why are you so afraid of the bear?" Josh asked.

Pitt sighed, grew silent, stared more intensely into the fire, and began telling his story.

CHAPTER TWELVE

"When me and Lor were married a couple years, I convinced her to go camping with me back here in these mountains. She'd never been here before, so it wasn't hard getting her to come along. She always wanted to see what was out here, she said. We drove in with old Tom on the same road we came up the other day and hiked in from the same trailhead. Tom said he wanted to show us a particular lake, said it was the most beautiful place he'd ever seen. So after a few days, we got into this valley we're in right now. In fact, we camped at this place right here before we went up the trail through a meadow just over the next ridge. That's as far as we got. A big sow cinnamon bear charged us out of nowhere while we were stopped to eat a bit of lunch. Tom's gun was on the ground, and Lor was closest to it, so she grabbed it and fired. The bear went down, but came up again on three legs. She surprised us by hobbling away into the bush, and we were scared she would charge again."

Pitt stopped and lowered his head, taking a deep breath.

"What happened next?"

"When we turned around, Tom was lying on the ground with a hole in his chest. It didn't make sense. We knew the bear was wounded, but the shot had hit Tom, and he was dying. I knelt down beside him, and all he had the strength to say was, "It wasn't..." I asked him, 'It wasn't what, Tom?' But he was gone."

"Lor was in shock. She kept telling me we needed to get him to water or to the lake, but he was dead. I hollowed out the ground as best I could with the small shovel I had in my pack. And I buried him there with a pile of rocks on top of his grave in the meadow. Lor and me went back to town. She didn't talk the whole way. She started drinking when we got home, and she kept at it pretty steady for a couple of years until she ended up in the hospital. I think she wanted to die. We couldn't talk about what happened, and sometimes I would just drink along with her."

"Didn't the police charge her?" Josh asked.

"I went to the cops right away and told them I did it. Told them it was a hunting accident. It was fall, elk season. I said the gun just went off when Tom handed it, butt first, to me. One of the cops, an older guy—he'd come to our house a few times when I was a kid and the old man had kicked me half to death—he knew me and Tom, and he didn't believe I would ever hurt Tom. There were no charges, and we're a small, remote town that most people don't care about. Tom had no family, and no one really cared much that he was dead. No one except me. I knew Lor cared, but she never said anything . . . and maybe that one cop cared a bit—he seemed to anyway. Me and Lor just drifted farther and farther apart, and I gave her lots of reasons not to want to talk to me about personal stuff."

"A few days after she . . . after Tom died, I went through the few papers he had in his place, and found a will. I showed it to a lawyer—guy named Switz—and he said it was a real will, all legal. And he said old Tom had left me his property and the contents of his cabin. I guess I was kind of like a son to Tom, and he was like a dad to me. But in a town like ours, where everybody knows everybody, people talk. Somebody started spreading the idea that I meant to kill Tom because I inherited his place."

"Did you tell anyone else what happened in the meadow?"

"Gracie knows. That's all. Well, maybe Switz knows now. I didn't like the way he was looking at Lor the day we took Tom's will to him. But things were already bad for us. I don't know when she started seeing him, but when I think back to that day, I realize I was too stubborn to think she would ever leave me."

"Ever figure out what happened—how a bullet killed Tom *and* hit the bear?"

"Must have ricocheted . . . that's all I can say . . . maybe hit a rock after going through Tom. It made an awful hole in him."

Pitt bowed his head and pulled his cap down and held it over his eyes. The memory burned like fire, and his own words had pulled it like a searing iron from where he had tried to bury it beside Tom's bones. He wanted to change the subject, to get away from the memories, to leave the past in that grave in the meadow. But he was going back there, drawn by some invisible cord. Why he was determined to find the lake that Tom had described was something he had trouble explaining even to himself, but the idea filled an empty place in his soul, and maybe, he thought, he would find a little peace there.

Lud was in his tent snoring, and the rhythmic sound was distraction enough. Although the valley was dark, the mountains were silhouetted against the sky that, during northern summers, turned gray-blue instead of black. Pitt gazed to the west, thinking he had never seen the peaks as they looked on this night.

"Something's different," he whispered to no one. "I see a different . . . ." He reached into his memory for the word, but finding none, he quietly stared at the misty, blue peaks.

"Dimension." Pitt was startled by the word. "Dimension," Josh repeated. "A different dimension." How Josh knew the word that Pitt was looking for was troubling, but he was becoming accustomed to the surprises. And Josh was right. Pitt was looking at the familiar for the first time, as if in a different dimension. But the reason why was unclear to him, and for the moment, the reason didn't matter.

"You ask why I'm afraid of the bear? I'm more angry than afraid. A thousand times I've wished I got killed that day in the meadow . . . at least a thousand. I'm a nobody goin' nowhere. I shouldn't have brought Lor up here, and Tom shouldn't have died. I'm less scared of the bear than I'm scared of life."

Neither said anything then. Each went to his tent, and Pitt slept the fitful sleep of exhaustion and fear. His was the sleep of a man who felt damned, who was convinced he was a failure, yet a man who still wanted to prove to someone, anyone, that he could be better.

In his dreams that night Pitt looked over the valley from the ridge above. The valley became a canyon, and in the bottom of the canyon a fire was raging, the flames reaching up to touch his face, forcing him to step back from the ridge. Then he was across the valley in the meadow, standing beside Tom's grave. The rocks covering the grave were moving; a large bear emerged from them and steadily moved toward Pitt, who was stepping back. He lifted his rifle and aimed at the bear's chest, but his hands were small and white. He tried to squeeze the trigger, and nothing happened. He tried to lever another shell into the chamber, but the gun jammed, and the bear kept coming until Pitt fell on to his back. A heavy paw rested on his chest, forcing the air from his lungs, crushing the life from him. For a moment, the bear became a dark figure, a shape more than a body, a suffocating silence, constricting his throat, paralyzing his limbs. He tried to scream, to call out for Lor, but no one was there to help. In a whisper, he called for Josh; the dark shadow fell back. Pitt could breathe again, and he awakened, wet with perspiration.

He lay still then, momentarily savoring the relief one feels when awakened from a nightmare yet remembering the panic that had held him moments before. And as he recalled the dream, he felt tired of living with fear, and more tired of hiding it behind a mask of anger and drowning it in a wash of whiskey. Not far away another man was lying still in his tent, but he was not thinking about a recent nightmare. He was planning the next one.

CHAPTER THIRTEEN

Early dawn in the Coastal Mountains pried open the grey canopy of night, revealing four men, each thinking he knew the plans for the new day, each expecting to fulfill his goal, only one aware of the cost. If someone had stood on the ridge from where Pitt, Lud, and Josh had descended, he would have seen three small tents as dots of color on the valley floor near the stream. Two men were moving near the tents. Four hundred yards away to the right he would have seen another small tent, further back from the stream, in a shallow draw that concealed it from everyone except someone observing from above. A half mile in the other direction, a thousand feet above the stream, the observer could have watched a man, who looked tall and thin even at such a distance, entering a large, sloping meadow, stopping to look down and to the west where the bulwark of rock and ice walled in the valley. And a watcher would see something else. Someone or something moved in the thick growth near the edge of the meadow, not far from a pile of rocks and two hundred yards from the tall man, who was still turned toward the valley. To the practiced eye, the brown moving object would raise concern and prompt the desire to warn the tall man of its presence.

But then another man appeared from the trees across the meadow from the tall man. He had a rifle on his back, and he walked directly toward the other man, who turned suddenly as the newcomer got closer. He extended a hand to the tall man, who quickly took it, and they shook hands briefly. They talked for a while. Then the man with the gun turned and left the meadow through the same place he had entered minutes earlier. The tall man at the edge of the meadow watched him leave and stood still for several minutes, looking in the direction the stranger had gone. He turned slowly and began descending the steep trail that led back toward the stream. And the observer would then see the cinnamon bear emerge into the meadow in plain sight.

Back down near the three tents, Pitt and Josh were nursing a small campfire, built from shavings Josh had carved from the driest side of a piece of deadwood. Both men were quiet as Pitt tried to forget their conversation from the previous night, and Josh seemed lost in thought. He had, as Pitt would say, his game face on.

As the days had passed, Pitt observed that Josh had become quieter and sometimes more aloof. This bothered Pitt, who had become familiar with the idea of having Josh around even if he did not really like him. Pitt wanted to ask if something was wrong or if something was bothering him, but to do so would be to expose the fact that he cared, to reveal that he needed a friend.

"Lud still sleeping off his concussion?" Pitt finally asked.

"Lud went walking early. He said he wanted to get some pictures."

"Of bears? He's nuts."

"I've got to go and find him. Pitt, wait here in case he comes back to camp."

"What for? He's a big boy." Pitt replied, chafing a little at the order to stay in camp.

"Not as big as he thinks."

Pitt watched Josh grab his pack and trudge with uncharacteristic effort up the trail.

"Where will we meet you if he comes back here?" Pitt called after him.

"I'll see you at the lake," he called back.

Pitt, who did not like most people, who preferred being by himself, who was out of booze and low on cigarettes, stood and watched the trail, wondering if he should go after Josh, because he had to admit that he was worried about him. But he knew how easily a man could get lost in these mountains, so he understood the logic of staying by the camp while Josh searched. He could deal with being out of alcohol. He was mostly a binge drinker. But rationing smokes was fraying his nerves as he continually battled his craving and habitually reached for his shirt pocket, only to find it empty because he had zipped his remaining cigarettes into his backpack.

He dug out a cigarette and sat down to poke at the fire, watching it turn to coals and smoke. The day was unusually warm; the sky was cloudless; the sun was already high. He looked across the smoldering wood at the old 44, and he thought about Tom. Soon, he thought, he would visit his old friend's grave and pay his respects. Although the meadow was far from his cabin, Pitt felt he was coming home when he got to the meadow. But it was also a sad place, a place Pitt feared, the end point of Tom's life and the only friendship Pitt had truly valued. Still, he looked forward to getting on to the meadow and then, finally, to the lake.

For years, he had thought of visiting the place that Tom described as peaceful, crossed with quiet streams, filled with wildlife. It was a large, oval-shaped meadow, more like a bowl one ascended into from the valley on the south end, surrounded on three sides by slopes, two covered with trees, one with rock and scree that rose up from a small tarn at the north end.

A sound suddenly drew his attention back to the small camp, and he was on his feet, squinting and listening intently in the direction where the noise had come from. Had it been an eagle screeching? As he stood still, he realized that the scream-like noise had gone on for several seconds before he had become aware of it. He heard it again, and he shivered from his core as he grabbed up his gun and then his pack and began moving quickly up the trail toward the sound. The sound was human. He levered a shell into the chamber of the 44 and un-cocked the hammer while he ran. The safety was off. He was certain that he ran toward danger.

At the base of the overgrown, barely visible switchbacks that led from the valley floor to the meadow, he met Lud, coming as quickly down as Pitt was going up. They met so unexpectedly that they collided, each almost knocking the other off his feet. For a second they grabbed each other for balance, then stepped back, wary of the contact.

"What's going on?" Pitt demanded.

"The bear . . ." Lud puffed, his breath coming in sharp gasps, his eyes looking large and ringed with fear, his voice betraying astonishment and panic.

"What about the bear?" Pitt demanded again, his own breath labored and his patience beyond spent.

"The bear . . . the old bear . . . got Josh. I didn't mean . . . I didn't think . . . I mean I didn't know they could move so fast. I pulled out my camera when I saw it digging for something near the edge of the meadow. I was taking pictures, and she charged. Josh stepped in front of me and she backed off at first, like she was bluffing. But then she came at us again, and I ran, but Josh stood still. I heard his scream, and when

I turned around, she had him by the arm and was dragging him away. He looked bitten up bad. He was like a rag doll. I think he's dead." He panted and stared at the ground.

"And you ran?" Pitt spat on the ground. "Start back to town. Don't stop. We'll need help." He watched as Lud, speechless for the first time, turned and headed back toward their camp, walking and then loping with an awkward gait. Pitt continued up the trail, walking now, calculating his options once he reached the meadow. The old bear must have felt surprised, he thought, or she just saw one man alone and decided he was a threat she should attack. Maybe she had a cub nearby.

Cresting the ridge at the edge of the meadow, he stopped. He scanned the trees and then eased forward with careful steps, never taking his eyes from the tall brush at the rim of the open space. He became aware that the meadow did not appear as he had imagined or remembered it. Behind him the valley sank deep between the meadow and the opposite ridge. Before him the space looked dry, almost alkaline in places. Around him the trees looked scrubby and stunted. Within him he felt the betrayal of memory, the deception of longing for the past, the foolishness of hoping to find something he had lost when what he lacked was the friend who made it worth remembering.

Maybe he felt helpless, maybe he felt afraid, maybe he felt desperate, but at the edge of the meadow in the long grass near a crude cross, beside Tom's grave, Pitt did something he had never done. He knelt and prayed. He asked for help, and he prayed for strength, and he pleaded for the life of the man he had to try and rescue. He stood then, knowing the odds were long and the chances slim, but he turned to the north without planning his route and started walking toward the shale on the edge of the meadow.

He picked up the trail not far from the trees, close to the rocky slope. The left, front track of the bear was turned slightly inward. So it was her. The grass was flattened by the dragging of Josh's body or corpse. He did not know which. Pitt's boots were soon red with blood as he waded in the crushed grass. His eyes forward, his rifle ready, his mouth dry, he willed each step, aware that he could come upon the bear at any moment. Sweat ran into his eyes. He adjusted his pack. He stole forward, and he thought he heard music but told himself it must be in his head. Why that song, and why now?

Then the tracks ended. She had walked on the shale. But Pitt could still see the blood, a lot of blood. To keep moving, to keep hunting the hunter, to keep looking for an old enemy, to keep searching for a new friend felt like a mission—like something he had been missing, like the end of one thing, yet the start of something else. And he felt sure he heard music again. He followed the blood trail back into the trees, stepping carefully to avoid cracking twigs, crouching cautiously to evade tangled branches. Then the scraggly forest opened again into another, smaller meadow. He stayed concealed by the trees, his breathing the loudest sound, his eyes the only things moving, taking in what he saw.

CHAPTER FOURTEEN

Pitt was alone and weak from hunger, which was a fact he had hidden from his companions. He had no more food, having packed for a shorter trip, having expected to travel alone and more quickly. In fact, he had expected to be back at the cabin by now. The only ammunition he had was in his gun; he'd lost the rest when he fell in the flooded stream along the trail. His only other protection was strapped to his side in the form of an 8-inch hunting knife. It was already Friday, and he had planned to be home by Thursday, but he hadn't planned on having slow companions.

He spotted the young, wild sheep feeding in the meadow. It flicked an ear to disturb an annoying fly, lifted a hind leg to scratch a tick from its belly, and otherwise seemed oblivious to Pitt's desperate heart rate that pounded in his ears like thunder. Without shifting his gaze from the sheep, he loosened the big knife from its sheath with his right hand. He was nervous. Where was the bear? He looked around the perimeter of the small meadow. The lamb had drifted closer, about ten feet away from the spruce trees that concealed Pitt.

Pitt was still hidden from its sight, and he was downwind. He admired the silky, shiny coat of the animal. Most mountain sheep he had seen were small, having fought tough winters and meager grass. The sheep moved closer. His muscles grew involuntarily tense. Then a sound pierced the air. It sounded like a woman shrieking in fear. He whirled to see where it came from just as the lamb did the same. But the cat was already on the lamb. The mountain lion's fangs sank into the back of the small animal's neck as the big cat's claws gripped its throat. The lamb tried to run, but the cat held on like a desperate cowboy. And the lamb went down with the cat still whining and growling through clenched teeth.

The attack was quick. Whether out of mercy for the hunted or anger at the hunter, he did not know. And he would never understand why he left his rifle leaning against a tree. But he plunged from the trees into the tall grass of the meadow, adrenaline fueling his brain until he reached the big cat still ripping at the spine of the downed lamb. He shouted and lifted his knife. The cat broke its grip but the damage had been done. The lamb was still alive but dying.

Pitt swung at the cat, but the lithe animal avoided his clumsy attack and was not about to give up its prize. With its ears back, it yowled from deep in its throat and as he swung again, it lunged at him and sank a claw into his forearm. He was bleeding, but the sight and smell of his blood ignited his rage with the result that he swung his knife at the cat's head. Suddenly, the fight ended and the cat backed away, looked past Pitt, then turned and ran out of the meadow and into the trees.

Pitt looked down. The lamb was still breathing with difficulty. He cautiously placed a hand on its head, and with his other hand drew his sharp blade across the animal's throat, ending its misery. In a moment, it was dead. He felt pity, relief, and then hunger.

Then he saw what the mountain lion had seen. The old cinnamon bear was bigger than he remembered, bigger than any he had come across in all his years in the back country. It stood on its back legs and sized up the man standing between it and the fresh kill. Back on all fours, it grunted at him, swung its head back and forth, and moved steadily toward him. His brain on full alert, Pitt held his ground, staring back into the eyes of the old death threat. Finally, here it was. Instinctively, he reached behind his back for the 44 but remembered that he had set it down when he approached the meadow, before he saw the sheep. When the lion attacked he had only thought of attack, not protection.

The bear came on as if she would run over him and take the sheep for her own. So this was it, Pitt thought. He would die in this place, and suddenly he knew he had nothing left to lose. But he would make it count, and he would leave a mark on the old sow. The dam of Pitt's rage burst against the thing he hated; he screamed, cursed the bear, and ran straight at her, swinging at her head. The point of his blade caught the bear on the nose, and she roared and reared up again. She was much taller than Pitt, but he was crazy with rage and pain. Something let go in his head. He roared and tried to stick his knife into the bear's broad chest, but the thick coat and bone structure allowed him little. Instead, the bigger creature batted him away with such force that he felt his left arm snap. He lay stunned for mere seconds in the grass, but as the bear came on, he sprang at her with the knife he had somehow managed to hold in his right hand. He squealed in pain as he thrust his broken arm into her jaws and throat and, swinging wildly with the knife in his right hand, he gouged the old animal in the left eye. She roared in pain, trying to bat away his arm, but she missed. Pitt kept on, stabbing at her face, until finally he thrust upwards into her neck with all his strength before she knocked him over with a powerful blow. She shook her head as, blinded and bleeding, she turned and limped out of the meadow. Pitt stood rigid with the knife hand stretched out, his chest heaving.

The bear disappeared into the forest, and Pitt's resolve drained away. He collapsed to his knees, aware of the odd angle at which his left arm stuck out from his body. Staring down at the wound that the lion had left in the same arm, he tried to muster enough strength to tear the sleeve from his shirt in order to bandage his masticated arm, but he was too weak. And as the shock wore off, the pain made him feel dizzy and sick. He gagged, then wretched, but his stomach was empty except for the bitter bile that rose in his throat.

He staggered to his feet and turned toward the spot where he had slain the lamb. He felt sick, confused, and delirious. He thought he heard the song again, but it ended suddenly, and his head hurt as he panted and tried to stay conscious.

"Gotcha!" Someone was behind him. Slowly and painfully, he shuffled and turned to face the stranger who was holding a gun, a 44, but not Tom's old gun.

"Remember me?" the man asked with a sullen smile. Pitt looked beyond the gun barrel into the eyes of the man who had been posing as Harvey Trudeau, the same man who had assaulted Amy Cain, the man Pitt had beaten so long ago.

"I know who you are Jonas Mulaire."

"That's funny!" Mulaire laughed. "That's the second time a man has said those words to me. And you will be the second man whose memory I erase on this mountain. Last time, I timed the shot just when your sweet Lor tried to shoot that old bear. You and that pretty woman of yours were too simple to figure it out." Pitt remembered wondering why the echo of the shot had cracked so loudly off the rocks that day.

"Anyway," Mulaire continued, "that was some fight, better than any hockey fight I've ever seen. But I'm out of time here, and I need to get back to town. Got an appointment with my lawyer. I think you know Mr. Switz? Well, that's not his real name, but it's what you call him."

The smallest of tremors vibrated in the earth, small stones splattered down the slope, and a cool breeze danced with the tree tops and was gone. But in spite of the tremor, neither man took his eyes off the other.

"Go ahead, moron," Pitt said. "Killing me will get you nothing, 'cause there's nothing left of me. But why did you kill Tom?"

"Well, that nice property of his. Don't you see? We're going to set up a resort there, just outside of pretty little Emerald."

"Who's we?"

"Just some associates, and now you're asking too many questions, especially for a man about to die."

"You're a murderer and a liar, Jonas Mulaire," Pitt said and spat at him, furious at the arrogance of the man who had bargained for a night with his mother. Mulaire laughed and lifted the rifle.

"Where do you want your new hole, boy?"

"Wherever you want it moron," Pitt sneered. "Give me what I've got coming, even though you're the dumbest excuse for a man I've ever seen. You kill from hiding. You killed a good man, a wise man. Tom didn't deserve to die, especially at the hand of a snake. I'll be dead, but you'll still be a moron."

"Maybe." Mulaire was no longer smiling, but angry. "But that property the old man left you will be a fine place for my new resort, and I think I've found a manager—fellow named Ludrow. Those hikes he's been taking, 'looking for bear' I think he told you? He's been letting me know where you camped so I could stay out of sight."

"Not always out of sight. I saw you down the trail when you had a fire among those rocks. Looked cozy . . . for a moron." Mulaire's eyes widened when Pitt told him that he had seen him. Pitt was thinking now, not willing to give up to the man who had taken his mentor and friend, not able to ignore the loss of Lor to this killer's lawyer. He needed to distract Mulaire; he needed time. Maybe, he thought, he had a chance, and he had nothing to lose for trying. "I thought I recognized you, but I wasn't sure. And your tweaked-out friend Ludrow kept you hidden from then on."

Footsteps crunched across the shale behind Mulaire, who twitched at the sound, but did not turn to look. Again the ground trembled. Then more footsteps. Pitt frowned and stared at something on the shale. The young sheep was walking across the slope. Mulaire turned for a quick glance.

Pitt gasped in pain as he leaped at the rifle barrel, trying to jar it from Mulaire's grasp while swinging his knife. Weak and injured, he missed. But the force of his right arm was enough to move the barrel aside and the weight of his body knocked the other man down while the rifle went off beside Pitt's ear, bursting his ear drum, setting his head spinning. Mulaire fell back hard and lost his grip on the gun, which clattered off to the side. Pinned under Pitt's weight, Mulaire struggled. The earth shook. They heard more footsteps, the rattling of a few fragments of rock, the sliding and scraping of many stones, then the roaring and cracking of the entire slope.

Pitt, with his right arm and his knees, pushed himself off Mulaire and, in a staggering run, moved away from the scree and into the meadow. Mulaire screamed, but the sound was snuffed immediately by tons of tallow flowing over his head and body, the landslide coming as far as Pitt's boots where he had fallen.

When Pitt awakened, he did not know how long he had lain unconscious. He grimaced as he looked at his mangled left arm. He tried to see the time, but his watch was gone. He heard something moving in the grass. The young sheep stood facing him with no gaping wounds but only scratches in its hair, signs that it had been in a scuffle. All its mortal wounds were healed. It stared into his eyes, and he felt afraid, yet less alone than he had ever felt. The lamb turned, its brown coat and white markings glistening in the sun, and it took a few steps before stopping for a long look back. It seemed to be waiting for him to follow.

Pitt felt finished. What remained of his strength seemed puny. But something or someone called him from deep inside—some voice whispered, inviting him, urging him to step forward—to go on, not with noble courage or resigned hopelessness but with something like humility, something that would not let him sulk in the face of his losses, would not let him give up. And from that small voice, he found strength to go on. He simply obeyed a prompting he did not understand yet recognized as right.

Slowly they moved out of the fireweed that grew thick at the edges of the meadow until, at the edge of the ring of trees, they took a thin trail that parted the undergrowth. He suddenly became aware that the knife was still in his hand, and he gripped it more tightly as he remembered both the cougar and the bear. But the lamb showed no sign of fear. It moved slowly but purposefully into the forest.

Minutes later they were out of the trees again and back on the shale slope but unable to see the meadow as they walked a steep sheep trail that inclined toward a high valley. Pitt had never seen this place, although he had been close to it each time he had hiked to the meadow. Light-headed, he fell to his knees, too exhausted to feel the shards of stone tear his flesh. The sheep was waiting for him. He staggered to his feet, and the animal waited until he was almost able to touch it. Then it trotted ahead as if knowing exactly where they should go.

The trail crisscrossed the slope three more times before rising steeply over a rocky ridge, then dipping down into the most beautiful, green bowl Pitt had ever seen. He took in the colors and the fragrance, but suddenly noticed that the lamb had gone. He looked in every direction, still clutching his knife. Then he saw the river.

Streams ran from far up the valley, from glaciers higher on the peaks until they merged far to his right in a river. The river was deep, yet swift and boisterous at the same time. Its power drew him. He turned and slowly moved closer until he plunged or was pushed—later he never could tell—and forced to the bottom, where he was rolled and tossed violently until the water spewed him into a lake. The frigid water shocked his senses, and he surfaced, flailing his right arm, trying to get to shore. But the lake was rimmed by a rock wall. He reached for the rock though it had no place to grasp. Somehow it seemed to hold him, lifting him to its crest in the warm sun where he was suddenly dry, and his clothes were warm and clean.

Then, he saw the bears: great, huge grizzlies with tall, humped front shoulders and broad faces foraging for berries in the bushes by the river. When they saw him, they turned to face him; he felt strangely unafraid. They turned away to face another he had not seen approaching.

It was the lamb, and it began to speak, but its words came out as music, and after a moment Pitt noticed he was dancing—dancing freely and easily to the sound—and he shook his head, because, in all his broken life, he had refused to dance with his wife, had always felt clumsy, had feared looking foolish. Then he noticed that he was not alone. Where the lamb had stood, he now saw Josh, somehow wounded yet well at the same time.

"What is this place?"

"This is the lake that Tom told you about."

Josh reached into the water with a cupped hand, scooped out water and poured it on a rock. As he poured the water, Josh spoke gentle but firm syllables that Pitt could not decipher. Suddenly, the rock shook and burst to life, and, when it did, music that sounded like water falls and a fragrance that smelled like spring erupted from it as it became a living soul. Josh roared with laughter, grabbed the being by the shoulders and began to dance with him.

"Hardened souls come to life!" he shouted, and the rocks split and bloomed into color and sound, as if an orchestra were blasting out notes and new life at the same time. All sounds blended into a song.

"The rocks cry out!" Josh shouted again, and he laughed like one might laugh when everything in life seemed good, when the final game was over and the cup was hoisted overhead and passed from winner to winner, or when a longed-for love finally flowered, replacing pain with nothing but potential and hope.

Pitt was speechless. He tried to say something, but his voice sounded higher, younger. Josh, who now looked much taller, reached for his hand, which he willingly offered. But when he saw his own hand, he quickly drew it back, staring at it, turning it, examining the palm and fingers of a young boy.

"What's happening to me?"

"You're finally growing up, little brother."

"What? What do you mean?" Pitt thought he should feel angry at Josh's words, but, as he looked up into his face, he saw only kindness.

"How does it feel?"

"Ah . . . it feels very strange. Why do I feel good? I should be scared."

"There is no fear in love. Look around. What else do you see?"

"I see you, and I see . . . Mom?"

She knelt in front of him, looking young, as she had that day in the kitchen years before, except that now she had no bruises on her face. Instead, she appeared healthier than he had ever remembered her. She held him as she had on that day, and she whispered something to him. Then she was gone.

"Wait!" he said.

"It's all right." It was Josh, looking him in the eye, but Josh was not kneeling. Pitt was back in his adult body. He felt childlike and happy, yet clumsy.

"What's happening?" Pitt asked.

"You can go back home. My time here is finished for now."

"But why? Where will you go?"

"Home. I've got some things to get ready."

"Who are you, Josh?"

"I'm the friend who is always near Pitt. Talk to Gracie. She knows me. Your mother knows me. Tom knows me." Then Pitt felt the exhaustion of the climb to the lake; he felt the pain of his mangled left arm; he moaned and fell asleep; and he dreamed of perfect music by a pristine lake.

CHAPTER FIFTEEN

Josh poured water on an angular rock that burst into an awkward dance and took shape as a man carrying something that looked like a stick. Miles away, Kelly Ludrow walked alone on the trail, and suddenly he felt as though a heavy weight lifted from his shoulders. He began singing, then stopped to look around, as if checking to see if anyone was listening. He began to walk more easily, and his pack felt lighter. He threw aside the walking stick he had picked up along the way. Must be the drugs, he thought, trying to understand why he felt as he did.

Lud pulled off his pack and retrieved a tiny bag of white powder. After arranging the powder in a thin line on his knife, he bent over it, but before he could inhale it a blast of wind scattered the cocaine in a million particles of dust. Ludrow stared at his knife and laughed freely and deeply, as he had never laughed. He shook the remaining powder over the bank, wiped his knife on his pants, picked up his pack, and jogged in the quiet stillness of a perfect day.

His energy renewed, he plunged on, a new plan forming in his newly cleared mind. Gravity helped his pace as he descended from the high country and from the top of the ridge by The Majestic. He thought he must be within cell phone range. He pulled out his phone and punched 911 with his thumb.

"911," the muffled voice said.

"Ah, hi. I need to report a bear attack in the mountains."

"Please state your name sir."

"Okay, ah, I'm Kelly Ludrow."

"What is your location?"

"I'm by The Majestic."

"Where?"

"The Majestic. You know. The big mountain on the way to Emerald Lake."

"Just a moment please."

"Yeah. Hurry, okay. My phone is dying here."

"Have you heard of a place called The Majestic," the dispatcher asked a middle-aged officer who was doing paperwork at a nearby desk. He thought for a moment.

"Yes, I have. Why?"

"I have a man on the phone, reporting a bear attack. Says he's at The Majestic . . ."

The officer jumped to his feet. He had not heard of Pitt's whereabouts for a week. That was unusual, and the officer had heard from Gracie of

Pitt's hike into the bush. Switz, the lawyer, had come to the police station, wearing a sling and reporting an assault. As a result, the officer had been looking for Pitt.

"Put him on speaker," the officer ordered the dispatcher.

"Sir, where did the bear attack take place?" the officer asked

"Up by a big meadow, way back in the mountains."

"Are you hurt?"

"No. Not me. This guy Josh, a guide. He's dead, I think, and another guy named Pitt went looking for him. I ran for help." Lud knew the last part had not been true when he had left the meadow, but it was true now. Something had happened; something had made him care.

"Where is Pitt now?"

"Ah, he's probably back up around the meadow somewhere."

"We'll call for a rescue helicopter. You get back to town. We will need to talk to you."

"Okay," Lud answered, but no one heard him. His battery was dead. As evening fell, he heard, then watched, a helicopter approach and fly up the valley.

Pitt opened his eyes. He was laying in the small meadow—rock and shale scattered around his feet. Josh was on one knee, looking down at him. "I thought you died . . . all the blood." Pitt said as he looked up at Josh. He saw a deep scar on Josh's face.

"Who says I didn't?" Josh replied. And Pitt drifted off somewhere between sleep and wakefulness.

The helicopter pilot put down in the meadow and with another EMT, jumped from the aircraft and ran toward the two men. The other EMT carried a light stretcher. Josh rose and stepped aside as they approached.

"Are you both injured?" the pilot asked.

"I'm fine, but he's badly hurt," Josh answered, gesturing toward Pitt.

"What happened?"

"A bear attacked him, but he stood his ground as best he could. Something spooked the bear, and it left." They worked quickly and transferred Pitt to the stretcher.

"You can ride up front with me," the pilot said to Josh.

"Thanks, but I need to pick up our equipment down the trail."

"You're sure you're all right?"

"Yes, sir. I'm fine. Just take care of Mr. Cain."

"Okay."

Josh watched the rotor gather speed and lift the men away. He walked up the sloping shale that had buried the body of Jonas Mulaire until he stood over the spot where the man had died. Mulaire who would have yet again been the killer had become the victim of a powerful landslide. But Josh would not celebrate the death, no matter how justified.

"I'll see you again someday," he said and walked away.

In the hospital, Pitt kept asking for Josh, fighting the staff until they strapped down his arms and legs. When they asked who he was talking about, he said, "Josh . . . the man at the lake. I danced . . ." The doctor and nurses in the emergency room looked at each other, then back at Pitt.

"Check his blood for drugs," the doctor said. Then Pitt gasped for breath, and the rhythm of his heart, visible on the monitor, went flat.

He lingered over his own body, seeing the scene from above, hearing the staccato commands of the doctor calling for paddles. Someone shouted, "Clear!" A light shone off to his right—a light that reminded him of the halogen lamps he had fixed to his dozer for night work, yet this was an incomparably brighter beam. He lifted his hands to shield his eyes and looked through a narrow doorway into a spacious room that seemed somehow like many rooms in one. He wanted to go through the door, and Josh was beside him, smiling and gesturing for him to go inside. He heard the same music he remembered hearing during the hail storm.

But he looked back to the room below. It looked dim and distant. Suddenly it was silent. A nurse was turning off the monitor. "8:45," he heard her say.

A note fell out of Pitt's pocket as a nurse picked up his clothes and stuffed them into a bag. The note was a barely legible scrawl, written by a barely conscious man. It said, *Lor, not you falt. Mulre shot Tom.*

"See that his wife gets his things and that note," the doctor said.

The E.R. nurse began disconnecting tubes and removing tie-down straps. She closed Pitt's eyes and covered his face.

"It's your decision," Josh said. Pitt looked at the crumpled note and his broken body, and he remembered the story his mother had told about another man whose body had been broken—a man who died but rose again. Pitt wanted to leave and go through the door, but he needed to see Lor. He looked again at Josh, who understood his hesitation. Josh nodded and gently helped him back to the gurney.

Kelly Ludrow could not believe the rescuers' report that Josh was alive and well.

"Are you on crack?" he asked them.

"Certainly not," the helicopter pilot answered curtly. "Are you?"

"Ah, not anymore," he said. "Sorry, just an expression." And quietly, he mumbled to himself,

"Must have been the drugs, but I thought I saw . . . ."
The officer in charge interrupted his thoughts.

"Mr. Ludrow, I will take your statement now."

"Oh boy . . . okay."

He told of the hike. He told of his addiction and his arrangement with Jonas Mulaire, his supplier and his boss.

"But on the way down the trail, something happened to me."

"What happened?" The middle-aged officer looked up from his writing pad.

"It's, ah, hard to explain."

"Try me."

And Lud tried to explain why he had thrown away the last of his cocaine. Some things are unseen to those who will not believe in them. So he told the detective, who accompanied the officer, what he knew of Mulaire, and he revealed his addiction as well as his role as an expendable tool of the underworld. But the officer put down his pen and listened to a story that sounded familiar, like the story of another young man, who thirty years earlier, had found or rather been found by a better way to live. Sergeant Molloy felt as though he was looking in the mirror at his younger self.

The nurse jumped back and gasped as the heart monitor beeped out a pulse. Pitt drew in a hoarse, deep breath and sat bolt upright on the gurney, his eyes wide open, looking around the room, then focusing on the nurse. He looked down at his arm, grimaced, and fell back against the mattress.

"I'm not done yet," he said weakly, trying to smile. "I've got some things to take care of. Where's Josh?"

His nurse paled, grabbed for the bed rail for support, and blurted out, "Wait right there!" before running from the room.

"I'm not going anywhere," he whispered with great effort, and he tried to laugh, but his head hurt too much.

Seconds later, the doctor rushed to the door and stopped abruptly, the nurse close behind. His eyes widened, and he stepped deliberately, almost reverently toward Pitt, his eyes riveted on him.

"We thought you were dead!" the doctor gasped.

"I saw a bright light and . . ." Pitt said as his voice faded away.

"Really?" they asked, almost in unison.

"Got any water? My mouth feels like cotton."

"Here." The nurse tried too quickly to pour a glass, her hand trembling, splattering water on the floor.

"Thanks," he managed to wheeze hoarsely. "I need to talk to my wife . . . I mean my ex-wife."

"We notified her that you died," the nurse replied.

"She'll be happy about that, I think, but I need to talk to her," he continued quietly.

"She's on her way. An officer delivered your note to her when he went to tell her you . . . died."

Pitt heard a sound in the hallway and glanced toward the door.

"Hey, Lor," he said weakly. He felt no anger as she walked tentatively toward his bed, holding the note, her face unreadable—neither compassionate nor cold, her eyes wide and her mouth open.

"They told me you were . . ." she whispered while standing just inside the doorway.

"Who says I wasn't?" He tried to laugh, but pain rippled from his head to his gut, and tears trickled from the corners of his eyes.

Instinctively, Lor snatched a tissue from a box on a tray and handed it to him. He tried to take it from her but fumbled and dropped it to the floor. She pulled out another and carefully, like one might approach a wounded animal or a known threat, reached over, gently wiping the tears from his face.

"Switz is gone Pitt. He took the savings and he tried to get the house. I'm sorry, but . . ."

"It's just money, Lor. We'll figure out the rest. I'm so . . ." Pitt fell asleep and dreamed of a place where the unthinkable could happen, where he had known one perfect friend—a place where a man could be changed.

EPILOGUE

A week after the death of Jonas Mulaire, the little congregation gathered in its downtown sanctuary to dutifully pay respect to the man they had only thought they knew. By this time several stories were circulating about Mulaire's identity. There were no mourners, nor was there a lunch following the service. Pitt Cain did not attend.

No one in Emerald Lake ever saw Josh again. But the town was never quite the same. The change that had come over Pitt may have been part of the reason. He recovered more quickly than his doctor thought possible. However, for the rest of his life, his left arm throbbed when the weather changed. Everyone said he was still tough as nails, but he never played hockey again, preferring to sit in the stands with Lor, saying his arm was too crippled to play the game.

Three months after the helicopter airlifted Pitt from the meadow, he and Lor renewed their vows, and the small storefront church was packed, many standing along the side walls of the sanctuary. Following the service, a dinner was served in the foyer of the rink.

"Saw Pitt the other day with Lor," Jonesie said one day at the coffee shop. "Man, he's still a big guy, but when he's with her, you could melt him and pour him into a bullet mold."

And one day, several months later, Pitt stood with Lorelai and Gracie at his father's grave. His old man had died suddenly on the same day that Pitt was flown from the meadow. The three stood quietly for a few minutes. Finally Pitt stepped forward and looked down at the simple slab engraved with his father's name.

"Mom told me I need to forgive you," he said. "So here I am."

Made in the USA
San Bernardino, CA
23 January 2018